WEIRD WILD WEST

AN IMPRINT OF
INDIANA UNIVERSITY PRESS

KEVEN MCQUEEN

WEIRD WILD WEST

TRUE TALES OF THE STRANGE AND GOTHIC

This book is a publication of

Quarry Books an imprint of
Indiana University Press
Office of Scholarly Publishing
Herman B Wells Library 350
1320 East 10th Street
Bloomington, Indiana 47405 USA

iupress.indiana.edu

© 2019 by Keven McQueen

All rights reserved
No part of this book may be reproduced or utilized in any form or by any means, electronic or mechanical, including photocopying and recording, or by any information storage and retrieval system, without permission in writing from the publisher.
The paper used in this publication meets the minimum requirements of the American National Standard for Information Sciences—Permanence of Paper for Printed Library Materials, ANSI Z39.48-1992.

Manufactured in the United States of America

Cataloging information is available from the Library of Congress.

ISBN 978-0-253-04366-5 (cloth)
ISBN 978-0-253-04367-2 (paperback)
ISBN 978-0-253-04368-9 (ebook)

1 2 3 4 5   23 22 21 20 19

*Dedicated again to nephews
Evan Holbrook; Blaine McQueen; Peyton, Logan, and Maddox Neikirk;
and nieces Elizabeth McQueen and Amber Hughes.
Blessings upon you all!*

CONTENTS

	Acknowledgments	ix
1	Terrifying Texas	1
2	Odd Oklahoma	25
3	Nightmarish Nevada	37
4	Numinous North Dakota	41
5	Spooky South Dakota	47
6	Unusual Utah	51
7	Abnormal Arizona	68
8	Unnatural New Mexico	76
9	Incredible Idaho	83
10	Mysterious Montana	89
11	Creepy Colorado	100
12	Way Out Wyoming	118

13	Outlandish Oregon	125
14	Weird Washington	131
	Bibliography	151

ACKNOWLEDGMENTS

Duly Acknowledged!

Drema Colangelo; Gaile Sheppard Dempsey; Eastern Kentucky University Department of English; Eastern Kentucky University Interlibrary Loan Department (Stefanie Brooks, Heather Frith, Shelby Wills); Amy McQueen and Quentin Hawkins; Darrell and Swecia McQueen; Darren, Alison, and Elizabeth McQueen; Kyle McQueen; Michael, Lori, and Blaine McQueen and Evan Holbrook; Ashley Runyon and everyone at Indiana University Press; and Mia Temple. Also: The Sovereign.

If the reader is wondering where all the California stories are, they are in a separate volume titled *Creepy California*.

WEIRD WILD WEST

1

TERRIFYING TEXAS

Your Friendly Neighborhood Ax Murder Cult

"I believe that demons take advantage of the night to mislead the unwary—although, you know, I don't believe in them."

—EDGAR ALLAN POE

ON NOVEMBER 27, 1911, SIX MEMBERS OF A BLACK FAMILY WERE murdered in Lafayette, Louisiana. The killer entered the kitchen door of Norbert Randall's cabin and used an ax to slay the sleeping husband and wife, their infant, and their three sons. The only survivor was their daughter, who had spent the night with an aunt.

An arrest was made the next day: Clementine Bernarbet, also black, who claimed to be originally from Beaumont, Texas. Her shirtwaist and skirt, stained with blood and brains, were found at the scene, which police considered a pretty darn good clue. More bloodstained clothing was found in her room. Her brother Zepherin (Ferran for short) and two other persons were held as material witnesses.

The police hoped Clementine would talk once she was behind bars, and a few months later she certainly did!

On April 2, 1912, she told the sheriff and two deputies that she *personally* murdered the Randalls. Also, all five members of the Andrus family in Lafayette on February 23, 1911. Also, a family of four in Rayne. Oh yes, and another family of five in Crowley. But she said she had accomplices with the massacre in Crowley. She claimed that she performed all of this butchery with an ax.

The body count in each family murder differed in various news accounts, but if Clementine was telling the truth she had a hand in murdering from seventeen to twenty people *at least*, including babies, whom she said she killed so they would not know the pain of growing up as orphans.

This was sufficiently astonishing, but Clementine had more surprises. She confessed that there was an organized cult of black religious fanatics determined to wipe out entire families of their own race by the ax. In the words of the *New Orleans Daily Picayune*, their goal was to "carry out the work of extermination, all along the Southern Pacific Railroad, from New Orleans to San Francisco," especially in Louisiana and Texas. According to Clementine, in 1910 five blacks—two men and three women, including herself—visited a "hoodoo doctor" in New Iberia and got a charm guaranteed to protect them from discovery of any crimes they committed. The talisman was described as "two crossed needles, bound with thread and wrapped with red flannel and a few old rags." Thus fortified, they went on a murder spree with impunity.

(The enterprising salesman Clementine mentioned, Joseph Thibodeaux, was located. He was a respected man, well known in the region and affluent, who indignantly declared that he was a simple farmer. Yes, he said, as a side business he told fortunes using cards. Also, he could cure illnesses via roots and herbs. But he did not sell "candjer [conjure] bags" or any other charms. His name does not turn up in later reports, so evidently he was investigated and cleared.)

The five murderers had sworn allegiance to protect each other—evidently their faith in the charm was not a hundred percent—and therefore, Clementine said, she could not divulge her accomplices' names. Every now and then during her confession she would tantalize her questioners by saying, "Oh, I want to tell you something but I can't."

She added that three more families were marked for destruction and surely would have been hatcheted had she not been arrested, but she knew her "friends" would get them yet. She offered a few unsettling details: the three selected families lived near Lafayette and comprised thirteen people altogether. Blacks in the region reacted in exactly the same manner as the residents of New Orleans would a few years later when they had their own serial killer Axman to worry about: they locked doors and windows that previously had been left unsecured, and families stayed up all night listening for intruders. The *Picayune* reported on April 6, "Of course, apprehension is felt by the white people also and all take great precaution in making all fast and secure before retiring at night."

Clementine's confession of killing the Andrus family in Lafayette was especially disconcerting. Her elderly father, Raymond Bernarbet, already had been accused of the mass slaying, arrested, tried, and, in October 1912, convicted despite Clementine's earlier confession. His son, daughter, and first wife swore under oath that he was guilty, apparently to punish him for beating his wife and abandoning his family. In fact, he had come perilously close to being hanged.

Clementine had even left some of her clothing at the Andrus murder scene in February 1911, as she did nine months later at the Randall house—the clue that led to her arrest. Evidently she was in the habit of leaving her bloody clothes behind when she wiped out entire families. At the time, she convinced the police that her father had taken her clothing to the Andrus cabin to use to wipe off his hands after killing the family.

The lawmen found Clementine's story of a wide-ranging voodoo conspiracy hard to believe. On investigation, some parts seemed to be fiction. She contradicted herself: sometimes she said she murdered the four families by herself; at other times she said partners assisted; at still other times she said her cohorts merely watched while she murdered. When pressed, she said she couldn't remember her accomplices' names.

On the other hand, since February 1911 thirty-five blacks had been ax murdered in southwestern Louisiana and southeastern Texas. (Another estimate was forty dead in both states.) In San Antonio, an unknown perpetrator slaughtered the Louis Casaway (or Gasaway) family, numbering five, with an ax in March 1911.

Some of the murders had occurred mere weeks before Clementine was arrested. But other crimes that appeared to be part of the series occurred *after* she was safely behind bars: On January 20, 1912, someone killed all five members of the Felix Broussard family—including three children, one only three years old—in Lake Charles, Louisiana. The bodies were "badly mutilated" and their heads crushed. The perpetrator left an ax under a bed and cryptically penciled Psalm 9:12 on the cottage door: "When He maketh the inquisition for blood, He forgetteth not the cry of the humble human five." The killer added the final two words to the psalm. Was it a reference to the five victims? A newspaper account called the atrocity "the third wholesale Negro murder in this state within the past two months and the sixth within twelve months," making a total of at least twenty-six dead in Louisiana within a year.

On February 18, Ethel Love, her son, and her two daughters were bludgeoned in their sleep in Beaumont, Texas. The perpetrator or perpetrators left an ax behind. Calling it the seventh in a series of similar murders, the press noted, "As a rule the Negroes killed are obscure residents of small settlements and no motive can be assigned."

On the night of March 26, an ax murderer killed six blacks in the home of Ellen Monroe near Glidden, Texas: Mrs. Monroe, her four children, and a boarder named Lyle Funacune.

The crimes were so similar that it seemed the same person or persons committed them all. Clementine Bernarbet's wild allegations were supported by rumors of an underground fanatical black sect called the Church of Sacrifice, allegedly headed by Rev. King Harrison (some accounts call him Harris), whose members committed human sacrifice. In fact, Harrison was described as the head of the cult in January 1912, a few weeks after Clementine Bernarbet was arrested. An article on the Lake Charles massacre described above includes the line "the series of wholesale murders of Negro families in this state . . . are now believed to have been the work of religious fanatics, and the officers are holding the Rev. King Harris, a Negro preacher at Jennings, La., for further investigation. Harris heads a sect known as the 'sacrifice church.'" Clementine seemed only too happy to describe her role in the murders but was evasive as to the identities of her accomplices.

Police wondered: Was the Church of Sacrifice real? Were Clementine and her companions members? And if so, what was their motive? Nothing belonging to the families had been stolen; there was no evidence Clementine had grudges against any them. It seemed unthinkable, but was human sacrifice truly the motivation?

Much of Clementine's confession was uncorroborated, but some details were confirmed. She said she'd fired a pistol at Norbert Randall after killing him. His body bore a bullet wound as she described. She also claimed that after killing the Randalls, she saw Rev. King Harrison outside the cabin and warned him not to go inside, as there was a dead man within. He verified her statement. On the other hand, since Harrison was supposedly the head of the ax murder cult, one wonders how much credence should be placed on his word.

On April 5 the grand jury indicted Clementine for murdering the Randall family. She greeted the news with an indifferent shrug. On the same day, police arrested Ella Thebeau of Opelousas as a material witness. On April 6, they arrested Clementine's half-sister Pauline Bernarbet of Rayne, who as of late had been "acting suspiciously." A reporter described Pauline as "somewhat resembling Clementine [but] is far more intelligent looking and seems of a higher type morally." A black preacher named Thompson was also arrested, apparently on no more solid ground than that he had underlined Luke 3:9 in his Bible: "And now also the ax is laid unto the root of the trees: every tree therefore which bringeth not forth good fruit is hewn down, and cast into the fire."

Another arrest came on April 8: Valena Mabry, also called Irene, whom Clementine identified as one of the cultists who had accompanied her. Clementine had been referring to a companion called "Irene," and officers, previously unable to locate her, came to believe she was a figment of Clementine's imagination. But she turned out to be quite real and living at Bayou Vermilion, giving many the uncomfortable feeling that the story about the murder cult was true after all. Others thought Clementine had named Mabry out of spite—after all, she already had falsely blamed her own father for the murders she had committed and nearly got him executed. But there was no evidence linking Mabry to the crimes, and she was released.

At this juncture it is worthwhile to ask an obvious question: Was there really a murder cult, or was Clementine Bernarbet fabulating? Sheriff Lacoste expressed doubt. He felt that, at most, the crimes were committed by Clementine and an accomplice or two. Bernarbet's ever-changing story didn't enhance her credibility, nor did her unrestrained joy when investigators took at face value some of her statements that were later proven to be lies. It seemed unlikely that a lone woman could slay so many people all at once, especially with such a clumsy weapon as an ax. Wouldn't the other family members have woken up and fled when they heard the first victim being struck? And yet, at roughly the same time black families were being decimated in small towns in Texas and Louisiana and the aforementioned New Orleans Axman was attacking entire families of Italian grocers—and all evidence suggests he worked alone.

On the other hand, there was also evidence that the cult was a horrifying reality. As already noted, the slayings continued even after Clementine's arrest in November 1911. The massacres of the Broussard, Love, and Monroe families had occurred respectively in January, February, and March 1912. On the night of April 12, five members of William Burton's family, including his brother-in-law Leon Evers, were ax murdered at Burton's home in San Antonio. This time the killers stuck butcher knives in the adults' backs before escaping. The press thought it likely the work of "an organized band of fanatics" and noted that the Casaway family had been similarly murdered in the same neighborhood slightly over a year before. Understandably, the black population of southern Texas suffered paroxysms of terror in the wake of the Burton murders. It was reported that so many stopped going to work that there was a serious labor shortage. Anonymous letter writers sent terrorized people notes vowing they'd be next. A reporter who visited the black neighborhoods of Houston one night saw lights burning in all windows and family members taking turns guarding their domiciles with shotguns. Foolish indeed were persons who ventured outside at night; they were certain to be summarily stopped and impolitely questioned by police if lucky, by vigilantes if not.

However, after the Burton family massacre, the ax murders of black families in Louisiana and Texas came to an abrupt end. Perhaps someone out there realized the game was up and they'd better put the ax away for good; perhaps someone feared Clementine was about to tell all. A whole seven months passed before the final crime that seems to belong in the series: the ax murder of three members of the William Walmsley family, which occurred in Philadelphia, Mississippi, on November 22, 1912. A news report describes the scene: "Walmsley's wife, Sallie, and the young child were strewn out on the floor of the house, with gashes in their skulls." Mr. Walmsley's body was found a hundred yards from the house near a picket fence. He must have run away and was vainly trying to scale the fence when his killer caught up with him. He still clutched a broken picket. One reporter put two and two together: "The bloodthirsty crime is similar to those committed around Lake Charles, Crowley, Rayne and Lafayette, in which nearly a score of Negroes were put to death by blunt instruments or an ax, and for which Clementine Bernarbet ... has [confessed]."

The simplest explanation is that the murders committed before Clementine's arrest were done by her, with or without help from accomplices, and the ones that occurred afterward were perpetrated by a cult—just as she said!—or by copycats. What was her reason if not robbery or personal malice? In her earliest confession, she hinted at a grotesque motive. As related by a *Picayune* reporter in the April 2 edition: "She had a strong passion to fondle or embrace people at certain periods of the month, and when she killed the families in question she indulged in this to her heart's content. The officers say her detailed accounts of her acts were most vile and repulsive, and she maintained that it made no difference to her whether the victim was male or female. This feature of her story was confirmed by the peculiar arrangement of the bodies in several of her crimes."

The newspaper did not explain the phrase "the peculiar arrangement of the bodies." If we read behind the lines of the journalist's *very cautiously worded* explanation, it sounds as if Clementine's motive for murder was a sexual thrill if not outright necrophilia. This desire was hinted at again a few days before she went on trial: "In her examination by the [insanity] commission she gave no motive other than the gratification of her low sensual nature, which the physicians found to be strong and overmastering. All her victims were brained with an ax, after which she embraced the lifeless bodies and fondled over them."

Meanwhile, back in Lafayette, Clementine's brother Ferran was still in jail, as was a woman named Duce, whom Clementine claimed was a member in good standing of the cult—indeed, Clementine *now* said, Duce was the actual "Irene" she had named in her confession. (Presumably Valena Mabry, the first Irene, was set free.) Clementine's trial was scheduled for October 21, 1912, but instead on that day a panel of doctors on the lunacy board was appointed to give her a mental evaluation. They determined that she was "a moral degenerate" but legally sane. This meant that she stood a good chance of getting the death penalty if found guilty. Hearing this, she said philosophically, "They can only kill me once." (A few days before, she had said to a doctor, "I shall have at least this satisfaction when I go, that I sent a number ahead of me.")

Her trial began on October 24. Local blacks were so afraid of her that none attended. The Norbert Randall family murders were the only ones in the long series that yielded forensic evidence that could be tied to Clementine. She was tried specifically for killing Mrs. Randall, her gory clothes having been found at the scene. New Orleans chemist A. L. Metz determined that the blood and brain matter on the clothes were human and came from the Randalls. More such stained garments were found in her room. This evidence, including her confession, was deemed sufficient.

Clementine's attorney, John L. Kennedy, put on a spirited defense, hoping that at worst his client would go to an insane asylum. He pointed out that the Randalls' clothing and Clementine's were all mixed together when taken to Metz's lab, therefore resulting in what forensic experts today would call cross contamination. (However, it probably would not have affected the test results if the blood and brains on all the clothing had already dried when the evidence was collected—as it likely had, since the murders were not discovered until several hours after they occurred. Even if it could not be proven conclusively that the blood had come from the Randalls, the fact that it was human defied an innocent explanation.) Kennedy urged clemency on the grounds that Clementine had an "unfortunate birth" and grew up in a "degrading environment." Despite Kennedy's efforts, however, on October 25 she was found guilty of killing Mrs. Randall. The jury may have felt pressured into giving this verdict, as the black citizenry of Lafayette vowed they would lynch Clementine if she were acquitted.

But the all-male jury was reluctant to put a woman to death, as they nearly always were in those days before women could serve on juries, and they reached the verdict of guilty *without* capital punishment, which meant life imprisonment in the state penitentiary at Angola.

No one else went on trial for the seemingly endless sequence of homicides: not Clementine's brother Ferran or the alleged leader of the cult, Rev. Harrison, or the mysterious woman known as Duce. There is a troubling ambiguity as to how many murders Clementine committed, whether she had assistance, and whether the cult was real or fabricated. Also, one can't help feeling the evidence against her at her trial was far from ironclad. On the other hand, cult or no cult, she freely (and gleefully) confessed to ax murdering twenty fellow humans, give or take a few. She was known to have been "harshly treated," along with her siblings, by her father, so much so that they conspired to get him hanged for crimes he didn't commit. Perhaps childhood mistreatment planted the seed of her bloodlust. Clementine Bernarbet's story has been largely overlooked, but she ought to be famous as a stunning example of that rarest of criminological birds: a black female serial killer.

Texas Pastimes

A young man from Gainesville, Georgia, moved to an unnamed Texas town in autumn 1883, thinking he might make his fortune there. Instead he made only his misfortune.

When someone in town was murdered shortly after his arrival, suspicion fell on the Georgian. The night after the crime a knock woke him up. He opened the door and found thirty masked neighbors in the front yard. It was not a social call. They insisted he confess or be lynched; he protested his innocence and was dragged off into the forest.

He was tied to a stake. Masked Texans took shots at him, barely missing, to encourage a confession. None was forthcoming, so they "tortured [him] with knives" and burned him with firebrands. As the sun rose, sending its friendly beams upon the deserving and undeserving, the mob rode away, shouting a promise that the Georgian would remain tied to the stake until he starved.

There he remained for four days and four nights, with no food or drink but a surplus of hunger and frigid weather. One night a solitary man, heavily disguised, approached. The mysterious benefactor brought water and nourishment; his conscience must have bothered him but not enough to set the prisoner free.

At long last, on the seventh day, a disguised individual turned the Georgian loose. When he got back to his shack, he found that during his week of captivity the real murderer had been discovered and lynched. Perhaps the mob forgot that they had left the wrong man tied in the forest, or they considered it one of those little trivialities that crop up so often in life that are just not worth getting troubled over.

It was reported in the national press in February 1884 that the young Georgian had had quite enough and was moving back home.

John B. of Millican disapproved of his daughter Mollie's boyfriend, Arthur W., and suspected the lovers were eloping. His suspicions were confirmed when he tiptoed to the depot a little after 2:00 a.m. on the morning of April 9, 1896, and saw Mollie and Arthur preparing to board a Central train.

The elopers thought they were home free, but no sooner had they stepped on the platform than Mr. B. stepped out of the darkness and fatally shot his daughter through the breast. Then he shot Arthur through the neck.

Suicide was next on Mr. B.'s busy agenda. He went to his workplace, the Green and Olive rock quarry, to borrow a pistol. (No explanation as to why he didn't use his own; perhaps he was out of bullets.) Failing, John instead seized a box of dynamite from the powderhouse and carried it a hundred yards from the quarry's grounds. He sat on it and struck a match. The following explosion disturbed the dreams of many a sleeper in the vicinity. A reporter noted that there were "not enough fragments . . . to fill a cigar box."

Yes, John B. of Millican really disapproved of his daughter Mollie's boyfriend, Arthur.

East Dallas police heard screaming in a saloon early in the morning of December 3, 1900. Investigating, they found a flaming man sitting in a chair. Two men standing behind the bar were puffing cigars and watching serenely, as though such a thing were an everyday spectacle.

"Bring some water here quick!" said a policeman.

"Get it yourself," sneered one of the spectators. "Let him die. What's the use of worrying over him?"

An officer used his coat to snuff out the fire. The man was taken to the City Hospital, where he died four hours later. Before he passed to a much better place, the two less-than-helpful barflies were brought before him, but, blinded, he was unable to identify them.

So what was going on here, anyway? The burned man was identified as Peter B., a constable at Garland. Evidently someone slipped him a mickey in the saloon, and while he slept he was doused with turpentine and set aflame. The two saloonmen, proprietor Eugene F. and bartender J.W.C., were arrested and jailed for their own protection—a mob vowed to deal out a fiery death to both but left after the jailer fibbed that they had been sent to Fort Worth. Eugene and J. W. C. refused to divulge the motive for immolating a customer.

The pair were shipped to Fort Worth for real on December 4, a mob threatening all the while to burn them at the stake.

Eventually Will R., Will P., and Drew P. were also arrested. Eugene went on trial in the last week of February and was sentenced to death. His sentence was later commuted to life imprisonment. J. W. C. and Will R. both received life sentences; brothers Will and Drew P. turned state's evidence. Research has unearthed neither the saloon crowd's motive for such barbarity nor the reason for their antipathy toward poor Peter B.

Missionary Philip B. rode on horseback into Fagan, McMullen County, on Sunday, May 10, 1903, leading a mule toting a pack of Bibles. The local cowpunchers were immediately repelled by his "clerical garb," including a vest and a long black coat, but particularly by Philip's high silk hat. The same day, he rented a room in a saloon called Red Pete's Place, which was a mistake. He erred again when he held a revival in the street in front of the establishment, during which he offered his frank opinions on the morality of his audience.

Philip B. made a further error in judgment on May 11. By then, word had spread to neighboring communities, and the town was overrun with intoxicated roughnecks who wanted to take in the sight of the minister for themselves. They were quiet during his nightly sermon, but when Philip entered the saloon to go to his rented room, they followed. He stopped at the bar and, perhaps hoping to set an example, asked for a glass of lemonade. The bartender repeated the request in a mocking tone loud enough to draw the attention of everyone in the building.

"Give him some pigeon's milk!" shouted a witty cowboy.

Philip glared.

"Don't you like that?" asked the cowboy.

"No, I don't," retorted Philip.

"Then get him a bottle!"

Someone tried to lasso the itinerant minster's top hat. Then he made the final mistake in his long list of social blunders: he lost his temper and struck out at the surrounding toughs. He was set upon by twenty cowboys and beaten like a drum. In the melee, someone cracked Philip over the head with a six-shooter.

His skull was fractured. He never awoke; he died in his room on May 13. The next day the cowboys buried him in an unmarked grave on the outskirts of Fagan without a ceremony. It was said that the locals' hatred for Philip's choice of headgear was the main catalyst that led to his death.

Scrappin' Valley, located in Newton County on the Texas-Louisiana border, is today a pleasant and peaceful location. But it wasn't for nothing that it got its name. At one time it was famous for its many feuds and the tendency of the locals to settle matters without bothering to consult police or lawyers. A sheriff explained in 1935 that the residents of the area "have clung to their primitive, unwritten laws so tenaciously that killings have been committed and never reported to the county seat thirty-two miles away."

The incident that made the valley the focus of national attention originated in 1930 with the disappearance of Richard R. He wasn't reported missing until four years later. In November 1935, acting on a tip, the sheriff found Richard's skeleton buried in the middle of a highway. Further investigation revealed that he was murdered after he threatened to turn in a prominent moonshiner. Such impudence could not be allowed to stand, so Richard was punished Scrappin' Valley style: he was shot by three men, who then buried him alive in the road, where unsuspecting travelers drove over his remains.

Raymond H. made his living as a Depression-era iceman. He had a fling with a married woman, Mrs. H. L. M. of Rising Star. On May 1, 1933, Raymond felt he should put his competition out of the way permanently in the following manner, exceeded in its stupidity only by its heartlessness: he stabbed Mr. M. as the latter lay in bed; had romantic relations with Mrs. M. behind the bed as her husband lay dying; then took the corpse and secretly buried it with the help of several accomplices.

Three weeks later, Raymond started worrying that someone might eventually find Mr. M. His brilliant solution was to exhume the body and hang it from a tree on a farmer's property, believing that the finder would consider it a case of suicide. Two boys out hunting rabbits made the inevitable discovery, by which point Mr. M. was little more than a skeleton.

Someone talked, and on April 5, 1936, Raymond was sentenced to fifty years in prison. "I know you aren't guilty," cried Mrs. M., a remarkable statement considering the circumstances.

John A., a Groesbeck dairyman, was kidnapped on May 21, 1934. The next day his son received an apologetic note from the abductors. The note was a model of politeness that would have warmed the cockles of Emily Post's heart despite the awkward social situation: "Your old man is safe—excuse us, we got the wrong man." Police interpreted this to mean that the criminals had kidnapped John by accident, having intended to steal John's wealthy neighbor.

But John wasn't "safe" at all. On May 25, his body was dumped in a water tank near Groesbeck. There was a bullet in his head; his pockets had been turned inside out, suggesting his abductors had searched for valuables; he was gagged with a handkerchief; and a belt was looped around his neck. None of this made a dram of sense to investigators: The captors admitted they took the wrong man, but why then did they kill him? Since the kidnappers realized immediately their mistake, why did they hold John three or four days before shooting him?

Investigators were right to be suspicious; the kidnapping was a clumsy hoax intended to misdirect police from realizing the crime was an intentional murder. In December three conspirators—including a Houston hotel owner and John's own son and daughter—were arrested for murder.

A police escort had to take fifty-year-old George P. from the jail at Athens to an undisclosed location on March 14, 1936. The action was not unwarranted, for the following reasons.

The J. W. M. family had boarded at George's home. They had vanished on Thanksgiving Day, 1932. George could give no convincing reason for their disappearance and was arrested in September 1933, then released for lack of evidence.

He was arrested again in March 1936 and this time confessed that the missing family was dead. He told an unlikely story in which Mr. M. had come home intoxicated and killed his own family with a club. George claimed that Mr. M. had tried to bludgeon him too, but George had wrested the club away from his attacker and killed him instead. But what to do with all those bodies? Rather than inform the authorities, George said, he had placed all the deceased in a meat cooking vat, boiled the flesh off their bones, and then burned the bones. It had just seemed like a good idea at the time.

One part of his story was confirmed in spades, so to speak: George led the police to a site where a little digging turned up several cheery-looking skeletons.

Four on a Limb

Few crimes were considered more serious in the Old West than horse stealing, as illustrated by a spectacular lynching that occurred in Blue, Texas, on June 27, 1877. Fifteen masked men raided a dance and captured four men thought to be horse thieves: Wade Alsup, John Kuykendall, Young Floyd, and Blake Scott. They didn't have far to ride. A hundred yards from the festivities, the vigilantes threw ropes around the necks of the four men, who then did dancing of a very different sort while suspended from a tree limb. No doubt that broke up the party.

The next morning the lynched men's friends ventured to the tree to collect their bodies. A novel sight greeted them: The combined weight of the victims had bent the limb during the night. They were found standing under the limb with their feet on the ground, as though they were waiting for a passing stagecoach. The four were buried in a mass grave in Burns Cemetery.

The vigilantes had actually sought five men at the dance, but the fifth had escaped because he'd been using the privy when the lynching bee showed up.

Advance Notice

Maud C., described as "one of the most beautiful young ladies of Indianola," was visiting relatives in Victoria in July 1879. She baffled her friends in town by singing that creepy folk standard "See That My Grave Is Kept Clean." A few hours later, the nineteen-year-old took a six-shooter and gave reporters an opportunity to demonstrate how graphic nineteenth-century newspapers could be: "She literally blew her brains out, the whole front part of the skull being torn off. Miss C. fell on her back, her brains and blood being spattered all over the room." Then her friends understood Maud's cryptic choice of entertainment.

Work Shirkers

Being a laborer on a Depression-era Texas convict gang must not have been as much fun as it might sound, judging from two incidents that took place a month apart. On May 13, 1937, nineteen-year-old William S. paid two other cons five bucks to chop off his leg so he wouldn't have to do any more garden work. This occurred at the Harlem Prison Farm, now known as Jester State Prison Farm.

On June 11, prisoner Ernie B. decided anything was preferable to working in the hot summer sun at Eastham Prison Farm, so he found a rattlesnake and persecuted it until it bit him.

Leave 'em Laughing

Camilo Gonzales was hanged in Brackett on April 16, 1886, for murdering a rancher named Johnson on November 1, 1884. His nonchalance was the subject of much comment. He had slept well the night before his hanging, ate a hearty breakfast and lunch on the day of, "ascended the gallows with a firm tread," and even placed the noose around his own neck. (The sheriff removed and replaced it, perhaps figuring this was a task best left to experts.) Camilo made a speech asserting his innocence, waved gaily at his friends peeping through the jail windows, and, most memorably, enjoyed a good laugh as he dropped through the trap.

Sinkhole and Stinkhole

Two miles south of Marble Falls there is an aperture in the ground called Dead Man's Hole, seven feet in diameter and 155 feet deep—the perfect depth and width for disposing of an unwanted object, say something man-size. The hole got its evocative name because a few years after the Civil War at least seventeen bodies, and possibly as many as thirty-six, were found at the bottom and carefully extricated. It is thought they were pro-Union sympathizers who had been murdered. Three victims known to have unwillingly contributed to the site's name were Judge John R. Scott, Adolph Hoppe, and Ben McKeever.

The place is now a morbid tourist attraction complete with a state historical marker. According to Ron Franscell, author of *The Crime Buff's Guide to Outlaw Texas*, to this day a mephitic stink arises from the hole in the summertime, which suggests that some pieces and bitties may still be down there. Or maybe it's just natural gas.

A Hotel Fit for Ghosts

In 1890, Col. Elihu Harrison Ropes of New Jersey was convinced that the area around Corpus Christi was destined to become a great city. He was so sure of it that he purchased land there, imported a huge dredge to dig a deep channel through Mustang Island, and built a railroad that linked Corpus Christi with Brownsville.

At the same time, he constructed an enormous hotel for the throngs that he was certain would be attracted to the region. It was erected on a bluff overlooking Corpus Christi Bay, four miles south of town. According to Murphy Givens, local historian, author, and radio commentator, the location was "at Three-Mile Point on what is today Ocean Drive at Airheart Point."

Ropes's grandly named Alta Vista Hotel had over 100 rooms with hardwood floors, a grand staircase, and a third-floor ballroom made of walnut and expensive mahogany. The structure cost $125,000. (The modern equivalent would be over $3 million.)

The still-unfinished hotel was opened on August 14, 1891. Its glory days were stunted; just as it was completed, the Panic of 1893 put the kibosh on land speculation. Ropes had no choice but to go back to New Jersey. The Alta Vista stood improbably in the middle of nowhere, majestic and abandoned. In 1897, a reporter described it as being "situated in a big cattle pasture, and it is the home of bats and owls."

The building remained empty for fourteen years. J. J. Copley purchased it in 1907 and completed its construction. Like Colonel Ropes, he had big plans, according to Givens: "He built a bath-house and piers into the bay. A mule-drawn trolley ran from the downtown to the hotel." But then Copley went bankrupt as well. The hotel was briefly used as the Peacock Naval College in 1912. Then it closed, cementing the Alta Vista's reputation as a bad luck building.

A local named Theodore Fuller visited the place in 1916 and reported that it was loaded with famished and friendly fleas. The hotel, which knew only intermittent and fleeting moments of glory, burned to the ground in June 1927.

Timing is everything. Today Corpus Christi is a major metropolis, just as the unlucky Colonel Ropes predicted.

The Joy of Sects, or: No Sects with Men

One of the most unique and overlooked nineteenth-century religious groups in America was a Texas sect that consisted only of women. Formed at Belton in the mid-1870s, it was known variously as the Sanctificationists, the Sanctified Sisters, and the Belton Woman's Commonwealth. It has been pointed out that the sect was a haven for women who were victims of domestic abuse. They clung with tenacity to four major doctrines: (1) Share all property. (2) Isolation from the rest of the world. (3) Total celibacy. (4) No men allowed!

The sect was regarded by detractors as a glorified institution for homewreckers since so many members previously had been married and even borne children until they saw the appeal of Sanctificationism and moved to Belton. Some brought their offspring with them. The founder, Martha McWhirter, had been a married mother of twelve in her former life until she took up her new calling, very much against her husband's wishes.

Each member was expected to work. A reporter related in 1895: "In the early days of the society the women determined to raise money in order that the society might be self-supporting. Each employed a method of her own for accomplishing this result." One formerly wealthy woman was a woodcutter for the cause; others worked as domestic servants, and that included the founder's own daughter; some did laundry; others raised and sold produce. But whatever money they made all went into the sect's coffers.

At first the Sanctified Sisters dressed plainly and wore aprons and bonnets like Quaker women, but by 1895 they were permitted to wear "modern hats." The thirty-two members in 1895 lived in the Central Hotel in Belton, which they owned along with a number of other businesses and farms. They ran the hotel so successfully that they opened branches in the Texas towns of New York and Waco. They claimed their financial decisions were guided strictly by revelation. If so, revelation was very good to them. By the end of the century, the sect had an estimated $100,000 to $200,000 in their common treasury. (The modern equivalent would be between $2.5 million and $6 million.)

The Sisters wanted to make their community as self-sufficient as possible. One taught the children brought by formerly married members. The sect had their own blacksmith, a cobbler, and a dentist with her own office. They had no formal worship services, but each Sister was expected to perform a daily devotional exercise.

They seldom spoke to anyone on the outside and associated with others only insofar as business required. However, though isolated, they subscribed to a number of newspapers and had their own library. In 1903 the book collection was moved to a building that became the Belton public library.

The Sisters had their critics, who pointed out that, theoretically, all of the members had some measure of authority, but Mrs. McWhirter obviously dominated and therefore they were not as independent as they might be. Some onlookers bandied the charge that the Sisters were "a handful of weak women held together by one strong, shrewd woman," but an observer wrote in 1899 that most of the members were "bright, intelligent women" and added that since they had abandoned their homes and families and toiled at the commune for over twenty years, it was foolish to call their devotion "a passing whim."

While the Sisters were the object of much sneering and raillery at first, they eventually became accepted by the community. Around 1899 the Sisters moved away from Texas. Using their considerable savings, they opened a commune in Mount Pleasant, Maryland, which they called the Woman's Commonwealth of Washington, DC.

Sect leader Martha McWhirter died in 1904. It seems her force of will and leadership were essential to the group's survival. The ascetic combination of self-imposed isolation, communism, and physical abstinence eventually appealed only to the most fanatical members. A mere two years after McWhirter's death, only eighteen women were still at the commune. Their numbers dwindled with time, though they continued to run a farm in Maryland and a boardinghouse in DC. The last surviving member, Martha Scheble, died on the Maryland farm in 1983.

An Incompatible Traveling Companion

The citizens of Van Horn found something unusual in the desert on November 6, 1933: the nude body of a woman, with a battered head and a cord around her throat, who appeared to have been dragged a short distance by a car. No one had the slightest idea who she was. Investigators suspected Arthur W., who abandoned a tourist cabin in Pecos with suspicious abruptness, leaving behind a clothing cleaner's bill and a blood-smeared piece of iron. They tracked him to Port of Spain, Trinidad, but were unable to arrest him: the former Cleveland steel chemist had taken a job as a steward on the Canadian ship *Lady Nelson* and sailed away.

Nevertheless, he was arrested in and extradited from Trinidad in August 1934. He revealed that the mystery woman was Irene D., a wealthy thirty-year-old Cleveland widow. He also said that he would willingly confess "because the officers have been so darned nice to me."

So why had he murdered Irene? Well, it had been in self-defense. Also, she had been such an irritating companion when they'd taken a road trip out West! The murder was the culmination of "a series of petty quarrels and bickerings." If we believe Arthur, Irene carped every foot of the way from Cleveland to Los Angeles. She criticized Arthur's driving and complained about cattle in the road in Arizona.

At last they made it to LA, then turned around for the return trip. The nitpicking and nagging recommenced. By the time they made it to Phoenix, Arthur was so annoyed that he threatened to drop Irene off in Louisiana and let her make her way home as best she could. When they stopped to eat in Eastland, Texas, "she became irritated when some men stared at her in the dining room; and when we left, she launched into a tirade against men and said many things about her husband. I said I doubted some of them were true, and that made her even more angry."

At last they came to the outskirts of Fort Worth. According to Arthur, he merely asked Irene what time it was. Rather than tell him, she reached into the back seat, seized a package, and clobbered him with it. Arthur responded by hitting her three or four times with a small piece of iron that happened to be handy. He stopped the car, and they stepped out for some invigorating fresh air, which had no effect on her foul mood whatsoever. She attacked him; he replied in kind.

Up to this point Arthur's story was barely believable, but then it veered into the implausible.

Irene collapsed after taking a punch, said Arthur. Did he call for an ambulance or otherwise seek help? No, he carried her to the lawn of a nearby house and tied a cord around her neck (why?). Realizing she was dead (presumably), Arthur stuffed her in the car's trunk and drove with her ripening body for several hundred miles until he dumped her at Van Horn, which seemed as good a place as any. Before abandoning her, though, he cut off her clothes (why?). Then he went on to Pecos, where he checked in at that tourist cabin and left behind the incriminating cleaner's bill and the murder weapon.

On December 13, Arthur was judged guilty of murder and sentenced to ninety-nine years in prison, which gave him plenty of time to think up a better story.

Kumbaya

Two feudists named Bill Rose and Jesse Robinson killed each other in a gunfight in Jefferson on April 4, 1871. The sheriff taught them a postmortem lesson in brotherhood by having them buried side by side in Oakwood Cemetery with their gravestones linked by a chain. The conjoined cast-iron markers—which curiously resemble tree branches—are there to this day, spreading their silent message of fraternity and coexistence to the gladdened hearts of onlookers.

Local legend has it that their coffins are also chained together for eternity.

Homegrown Massacres

On the one hand, George Hassell, a thirty-nine-year-old Farwell rancher, killed and mutilated his wife, Susan, and eight stepchildren. On the other hand, George told investigators that he had no idea why he did it.

Police were pretty sure that George *did* know why, especially since he had displayed premeditation. In early December 1926, his family had disappeared; he had explained to neighbors that they had moved in with relatives in Oklahoma. A week later, he'd sold his property for $1,500 and announced that he would be moving too. Suspicious neighbors called the cops, who brought George in for questioning. He cast further suspicion on himself when he stabbed himself three times in the chest with a pocket knife after police asked him pointed and uncomfortable questions about his family's whereabouts.

As George recuperated in the hospital on Christmas Eve, police found the bodies of all nine family members, along with a blood-encrusted ax, in the ranch's root cellar, located only ten feet from the kitchen door. According to one source, the youngest victim had been strangled, the oldest one shot, and all the others bludgeoned with the ax. Other sources contradictorily claim that George's victims were killed by straight razor or hammer. Presumably, by the time the remains were found they were in such a fermented state that exact causes of death were uncertain.

George admitted that his homegrown massacre had occurred on December 8. He had carefully positioned the bodies in the cellar. The oldest son was sitting up in a corner; the mother and three youngest children were placed together in another corner; and the others were lined up on the floor.

As a peculiar side note, George had married his brother's widow, so his stepchildren were also his nieces and nephews. His brother had been killed by a mule's kick as he'd toiled in an Oklahoma field—or so said George, who happened to be there at the time. Understandably, authorities considered reopening an investigation into this death.

George was a man of many surprises. On December 27, he said he had a confession to make. Authorities expected him to explain why he had killed his family; instead, he said that he had also murdered a woman and her three children in California years before. He gloatingly refused to divulge their names: "It was a good job and no one will ever know."

The next day he gave insight into why he had wiped out his family. Susan had accused him of being intimate with her oldest daughter. Rather than answer the charge one way or the other, George had struck Susan with a hammer ("Where it came from, I do not know," he said—it must have been one of those magic hammers that spontaneously generate out of thin air). Then he strangled the youngest child and figured what the heck, he might as well kill everyone else too while he was at it.

As for George's other confessed crime, police inspected a house he had rented in Whittier, California, in 1917 under the alias G. Baker. On

February 1, 1927, they found the bones of four humans buried in the cellar. It was believed these were the remains of Marie V. of Pittsburgh and her three adopted children, all of whom had disappeared several years before. George claimed to be delighted by the find and issued a remarkable statement: "I am glad they found the bodies. They know now that I told the truth. I was afraid that when the bodies were found that somebody else might be accused of the murders, and that would be awful." One wonders: If big-hearted George was so worried that an innocent man might take the rap for his crime, why didn't he just tell the police right away where his earlier victims were buried?

On February 10, 1928, rancher George sat in a very special chair in Huntsville and discovered firsthand why Texas had a longstanding reputation for not coddling murderers.

In 1935, Lillie May C. of Center killed her husband, Robert, while he slept. She went on trial and got lots of unwanted attention that she deeply resented but which she would not have received if she hadn't murdered him. She maintained that she had done it for her children's sake: Robert was a bootlegger and thus a bad influence, and she'd had to "sacrifice him or the children." One can't help thinking there might have been other options available. Her silly argument won the day, however, and Lillie May got a five-year suspended sentence.

Nobody seemed to think it a bad idea to allow a murderess to go home to her children, about whom she had already expressed thoughts of "sacrificing." At least not until March 16, 1938, when she shot six of her nine children, ranging in age from five to thirteen, in their sleep, one by one. She kissed each good-bye first, so that's a point in her favor. She allowed her sixteen-year-old son, Travis, to live "because he could take care of himself." The other two survivors were a married daughter who lived elsewhere and a son who was visiting his grandfather the night Mom lost it.

Lillie May appears to have resigned herself to receiving attention from the press because this time around she willingly posed for reporters' photos. She stated that she was sorry now that she had exterminated nearly all of her family and rather wished she hadn't. When asked about her motive, she explained that she was "unable to provide for them." The financial burden might have been less if her husband had been still around to contribute.

Some cynics who were not apt to take her word for it noted that the family did not seem to be particularly poor, and investigators found a trunkful of clippings about murder cases. So it seems Lillie may just have had murder on the brain. Whatever her motive, on April 6 she was sentenced to 495 years in jail for her murder spree. The judge might as well have given her an extra five years and rounded the sentence off to an even half a millennium.

There were copycat crimes then as well as now. Only a day after Lillie May hit the headlines, Jane R., another resident of Center, tied up her seven-year-old son, threw him down a well, and jumped in after him. He survived; she didn't.

Nail Rain

On the night of October 12, 1888, Mrs. S. Schreiber was tending the lighthouse at Point Isabel, Brownsville—her husband, the regular keeper, had died recently—when she got a delightful surprise in the form of a rain of shingle nails.

The standard explanation for such strange precipitations is that a tornado some distance away sent debris aloft through the atmosphere until it reached an unsuspecting community, which then got a deluge of frogs, fish, grasshoppers, or what have you. The explanation would make sense in this case too, except that Mrs. Schreiber got another nail rain the next night. Dirt clods and oyster shells fell too, but mostly nails. And then it happened again on the night of October 14, "brickbats being added to the nails and oyster shells, and every now and then an old scrap of copper or iron casting," according to the town's correspondent for the *St. Louis Globe-Democrat*. Several witnesses, including Judge Lightburn, were walloped by the debris. A crowd gathered; the sheriff investigated, but no one could find the source of the material.

The event reoccurred on the night of October 15, when Mrs. Schreiber's house was pelted with bricks, dirt clods, mud, and nails. Unable to stand it any longer, she took refuge in the home of Rio Grande Railroad station agent Egan—and then Egan's home received the mud rain. "A strong force was organized," said the newspaper correspondent, "but though a strict search was made, the source from which the missiles came could not be discovered." The local mariners blamed ghosts.

Apparently, the phenomenon stopped after the October 15. If a tornado were the culprit, one might expect a greater variety of falling junk, such as boards, pieces of tin, hay bales, and the occasional farmer. Interestingly, too, Thomas Grazulis's authoritative *Significant Tornadoes* mentions no such storms in Texas in all of October 1888. Adding further mystery was that a decade before, County Clerk Glaenecke's house also had been bombarded by such unlikely debris, and all efforts to discover their source came to naught.

Keeping the Peace

A fight broke out at a dance held by black residents of Brenham on November 8, 1891; a couple of days later, two of the troublemakers were found hanging from a tree on the Yegua River near Blake's Crossing, lynched by the other partygoers. The vigilantes must have had only one rope handy, since both men dangled from the same one, "locked in each other's arms." Ironically, considering that all the trouble had started at a dance, they sort of looked like they were dancing.

Snowing the Officers

On December 8, 1925, the town of Stephenville was repulsed when hunting dogs sniffed out a disembodied head in the cellar of a razed house on the Riggs farm, twelve miles from town. Authorities placed the head in a bowl of formaldehyde and put it on display at the courthouse so that it might be identified and justice served. Someone thought it looked an awful like Bernie Connelly, a nineteen-year-old who recently had disappeared.

Connelly's stepfather, forty-six-year-old woodcutter Francis M. Snow, abruptly sold his gun after the discovery. The police brought him in for questioning, and on December 12 he admitted his guilt. The more they let him talk, the more improbable Snow's confession became. The dialogue between the killer and his interrogators, including the local constabulary and members of the Texas Rangers, is paraphrased as follows.

> **LAW ENFORCEMENT OFFICERS:** We see that you happen to be wearing Bernie's raincoat.
>
> **SNOW:** Oh, he traded it for mine.
>
> **LEO:** So did you kill him?
>
> **SNOW:** Okay, I admit that on November 30 I killed him, but only in self-defense. He attacked me in our farmhouse.
>
> **LEO:** Why didn't you call the police afterward? If you killed him in self-defense, wouldn't that have been sufficient? Why did you behead Bernie, haul his body several miles, and hide his head in that abandoned cellar?
>
> **SNOW:** Well, I can't rightly say! I must have been crazy!
>
> **LEO:** That explains the bloodstained ax and wagon we found on your property, but there's another sensitive matter we must bring up. Your wife and mother-in-law also have been missing since November 27. Did you kill them too?

SNOW: Uhh, they went to Waco three days before I killed Bernie.

LEO: We found human bones in your fireplace and in an ash heap on your farm.

SNOW: Okay, I admit I killed my wife and mother-in-law too, and I burned their bones. But it was an accident, sort of. After Bernie attacked me, I shot him with a revolver, and then my wife got mad, and I had to shoot her with the rifle. And the bullet passed right through her body and killed my mother-in-law, Mrs. Old, who was standing nearby. First I hid them under the cabin floor, but after Bernie's head was found I thought it would be smarter to burn them.

For *some* reason Snow's story of self-defense was not generally believed, and he went to the electric chair on August 12, 1927. Snow's cabin where the triple murder occurred was preserved and is now at the Stephenville Historical House Museum.

A Wooly Death

A female inmate at Austin's lunatic asylum died on July 17, 1888. The autopsy revealed that she had swallowed a hank of hair ten inches long, more than an inch in diameter, and "twisted like a chignon." This python-like ponytail was found in her intestine; no word as to whether it was her own hair. If not, how did she contrive to get hold of someone else's hair?

You Can't Put One over on the *New York Times*!

In March 1899, three men were lynched in Bowie County—or it may have been in Little River County, Arkansas, since it occurred so close to the Texarkana border. In any case, the inquest was held by a Texas justice of the peace on March 24. The coroner's jury's verdict was priceless, considering that the deceased had been hanged: "[The men] came to their death from natural causes, or were frozen to death."

The *New York Times* opined that this was intended to be a joke of some sort.

Hill of Heads

What are we to make of the report published in the *New York Times* of December 29, 1892, claiming that a mound covered entirely with human skulls had been found twenty-five miles south of Currizo Springs, near the road to Encinal? The mound was described as circular, "oval-topped," a hundred feet high, "and joined on one side to a short range of hills of about the same height." From a distance the mound appeared to be covered with round rocks, but closer inspection revealed that the spheres were "petrified human skulls distorted into grotesque shapes," their eye sockets, nasal apertures, and mouths full of sand and dirt. A worthy subject for a biker tattoo, to be sure!

There was contemporary talk of opening the mound to see what other nameless horrors might be inside it, but there is no record that this was done, and it might be just as well.

2

ODD OKLAHOMA

Premature Burial

John Stink (yes, really) was an Osage Indian who made a fortune from oil rights. He was also a notorious misanthrope who shunned even members of his own tribe. His antipathy for his fellow man originated in the 1860s, when he appeared to have died of smallpox. The medicine men declared him dead and buried him under a pile of rocks. Then they divided his ponies.

But John was merely comatose. After he wriggled his way out of the cairn and staggered home, the medicine men refused to return his horses, stating that he obviously was a ghost and therefore no longer needed them. Then, to add nomenclatorial insult to premature burial injury, they called the tribesman previously known as John Go-After-Fish "John Stink." The name stuck, as such names usually will.

The experience embittered John Stink forever (and his new name probably didn't help). Nearly fifty years later, on September 16, 1938, he died at age eighty at Pawhuska. He didn't climb out of his second grave.

Moon's Mania

W. J. Moon, a wealthy merchant of Caddo, went to St. Louis in October 1904 to purchase stock for his mammoth emporium. While he was away, his wife, Mollie, committed suicide. No one knew how to contact Moon, so Mollie's relatives had her embalmed and buried in Gethsemane Cemetery. The merchant came home three days after the funeral and demanded that

Mollie be exhumed and reburied according to his specifications. This was done.

Scarcely had Mollie been buried for the second time when Moon had her dug up again and given another funeral. He requested the women who prepared Mollie's body for burial number two to repeat the procedure for funeral number three. They acquiesced, but they didn't like it.

Two weeks later Mr. Moon decided to unearth and rebury Mollie again. This time around, what little help Moon could employ quickly deserted him and left him to perform cleanings and rituals by himself. "Moon seems to be perfectly rational on all other subjects," remarked a news article.

Moon finally realized that he couldn't keep vacating his wife from her sacred resting place any time he felt like it. He compromised—sort of—by having the poor woman's embalmed remains placed in a $500 coffin with a glass lid, which was housed in a brick mausoleum. Her diamond rings, gold watch, and other jewelry were clearly visible. Anyone who wanted to could enter the crypt and contemplate Mollie. Caddo author Mary Maurer quoted a woman who did precisely that: "One local told me that she remembers going into the mausoleum when she was fourteen. 'I was too frightened to see much,' she said. 'I can remember a glass covered casket, with a lady with long hair. It wasn't skeletal remains, but skin covered. Looked kinda like dried to the bone. My mother would have killed me if she had known I was there!'"

Mr. Moon visited the mausoleum every day to comb Mollie's hair and change her dress and shoes. After a while he hired a caretaker to perform these domestic pleasantries. Mrs. Maurer wrote: "The Moon mausoleum was open to the public for many years. The caretaker would take visitors to see Mrs. Moon and he would talk to her and wind her watch. After a rabbit died inside the mausoleum Mr. Moon decided to have a lock placed on the door. But the caretaker continued to unlock it for people. Years later vandalism forced [Moon's granddaughter Valentine Moon Craig] to have it sealed entirely. Bars were placed on the windows and the door welded shut."

W. J. Moon died on August 31, 1923. His third wife was kind enough to place his body in the brick mausoleum alongside Mollie. He was buried only once.

A Profound Disappointment

Wiley K., a wealthy Indian, was buried near Brazil, Oklahoma, in the 1860s. Supposedly, his will directed that he be interred with a large amount of money. On November 29, 1912, Rev. G. W. A. was convicted at

Poteau for unlawfully opening K.'s grave. It stands to reason that there was no treasure in the tomb—at any rate, the reverend was unable to buy his way out of trouble.

Necessity Is the Mother of Invention

Chief Crazy Horse of the Pawnee (not the famous Sioux warrior of the same name) believed he had created medicine that would make one bulletproof. Not being a dummy—perhaps he should have been named Not-So-Crazy Horse—he tried it out on his brother in front of the Council of Chiefs on January 13, 1896, at Perry. The council was far from impressed with the outcome and confiscated Crazy Horse's cattle and ponies as a penalty.

Max D., a twenty-six-year-old student inventor from Tulsa, devised a clever way to annihilate himself on February 22, 1932. He placed two handkerchiefs soaked in chemicals in a boxlike apparatus, placed the box over his head, and locked it. He was found asphyxiated in his attic laboratory.

Fred L., a farmer who lived in Dacoma, was troubled with a dislocated neck vertebra. He created a device he thought might "stretch his neck": a harness attached to a board that swung from the ceiling by a chain. In other words, a homemade gallows. Fred put his head in the harness and tried out his contraption for the first and last time on March 7, 1939.

The Downside of Pioneer Life, Part One

It wasn't always like *Little House*.

Something horrific occurred at Cross, near Guthrie, in what was then called Oklahoma Territory. On February 11, 1894, the region was crippled by one of the worst blizzards it had ever known. Many stories of hardship and death came in the wake of the storm, but none more horrible than the fate of the Sherman S. family, homesteaders who attempted to ride out the snowstorm in a mere tent. On February 12, rescuers found Sherman, his wife, and their five children frozen near a stove. All had their throats cut except Sherman's wife. A note beside Sherman explained all: "Wood all gone; Mollie frozen to death; the rest of us freezing. I have killed my family and now kill myself to prevent further suffering. God have mercy on us."

A Real Sense of Comedy Timing

Mrs. Samuel B. was giving birth at her home near Speermore on December 16, 1913.

"Well, old boy, congratulations," said the doctor to Mr. B.

"What is it, a boy or a girl?"

"Twins!"

Mr. B. dropped dead on the spot.

Theatrical Realism

A theatrical stock company visiting Clinton was scheduled to perform a play that required a prop electric chair. Somehow the chair was accidentally connected with a 2,800 volt wire, as the company's electrician discovered when he touched it on May 25, 1917.

Sincerely, the Corpse

Lt. William C.'s riderless horse walked onto the grounds at Fort Sill on November 22, 1936. Inside a dispatch bag tied to the saddle was a suicide note with a map giving directions to William's body and a request that he be cremated and the ashes scattered on the Centralia, Illinois, grave of his recently deceased sweetheart, Josephine L.

The lieutenant signed the note "The Corpse."

Skinned Alive!

In December 1933, Mr. W. J. Richardson of Eureka, Kansas, sent a letter to the *Louisville Courier-Journal* relating a horrifying true story his father had told him seventy years before about pioneers allegedly from Jennings County, Indiana, who set out for California at the onset of the Gold Rush. One of the party was an obnoxious bully who vowed to shoot the first Indian he saw. His companions told him in no uncertain terms that it would be an idiotic, needless provocation. Nevertheless, once they crossed into the Indians' territory the man shot a defenseless native woman washing clothes at a creek.

The anticipated trouble was not long in coming. A band of Indians surrounded the miners' camp and demanded that they hand over the killer—or else every man in the party would be scalped and killed. The miners sensibly pointed out the culprit, whom the tribe then skinned alive. As Richardson recalled the denouement of his father's story, "Soon after they got him skinned, he got up and walked back to camp and then fell and expired."

Some years after hearing this tale, Richardson wrote, he happened to relate it to a man from Louisville who remarked, "That man was my own cousin." Richardson wrote to the *Courier-Journal* to ask if any readers knew the name of this long-dead villain who had been parted so memorably from his epidermis.

A few days later, the newspaper printed a response from Ozema Whitlow of Elkton, Kentucky, who remembered hearing the same lovely story from her mother. She added a few details: the trigger-happy punk was only eighteen years old; she thought he was from Carlinville, Illinois; and he had long been noted for his sadistic streak. Even as a boy he had tortured animals and gotten a kick from slicing open frogs and lizards and smearing salt on them. Unfortunately, she couldn't remember his name either.

Now, thanks to the magic of backbreaking research, the whole story can be told.

Silas Claiborne Turnbo (1844–1925), author of several manuscripts on Missouri and Arkansas history, got details about the incident when interviewing Capt. A. S. Wood, an old Confederate soldier, in Marion County, Arkansas, in the 1890s. The *Courier-Journal*'s correspondent Richardson was mistaken in his belief that the pioneers had set out from Indiana; in fact, they had come from northern Arkansas. The year was 1853, and the fool who thirsted to kill an Indian without provocation was John Mankins of Marion County, "a large man [who was] quite overbearing and disagreeable." Turnbo wrote, "Before reaching the frontiers, Mankins made many boasts that he would shoot the first of the Indian race he saw; be it man, woman or child. The man repeated these threats so frequently after arriving on the frontiers that the remainder of the party grew alarmed and tried to induce him to not do so for fear the entire party would be massacred."

The miners arrived at a reservation on a day when all the warriors were out hunting. Emboldened, Mankins shot a woman as described above, much to the disgust and fear of the other pioneers: "The other emigrants deplored the cold blooded wicked act of the heartless man. They knew the tribe would avenge the death of the woman." They got out of the area as quickly as possible, dreading an attack that could occur at any moment.

Their apprehension was not unfounded. Four days later, they saw a hundred mounted Indians coming their way wearing war paint, a detail that did not bode well. The Indians requested that the woman's murderer be delivered or they would avenge themselves on everyone in the party. Not being dummies, the miners complied: "Mankins had committed such a wicked murder that they had no sympathy for him and they handed him over at once." (Also, they were outnumbered.) "The prisoner knew he was doomed to a terrible fate and the trembling wretch begged and implored the white men to save him from the vengeance of the red men, but his pleading was in vain. He had brought it on himself; he would have to pay the penalty that suited the desire and thirst of the warriors."

What the Indians had in mind for Mankins wasn't exactly a bed of hollyhocks. Turnbo described how the tribe forced him to taste his own sadistic medicine:

> The Indians . . . bound the man head and foot to one of the hind wheels of a wagon. The Indians did not delay much time in preliminaries when they examined their knives to see that they had keen edges and the awful scene of flaying a man alive began; they began at the neck and the man's blood was soon flowing little streams down his nude body for they had stripped him of all his clothes before they tied him to the wheel. They slowly but surely took the skin from his entire body not in small bits or strips, but whole. The awful torture was done in the presence of the white men. Mankins struggled and screamed in agony, his suffering was terrible and miserable; he begged, prayed, and cursed. The bloody work went on. The unbearable torture was continued. The man had cruelly murdered a poor defenseless Indian woman, and the tribe she belonged to were punishing him with the worst torture they could devise.

Mankins survived for an hour. The tribe stayed on the scene until he died and then galloped home, war whooping and carrying away Mankins's pelt as a souvenir. The miners buried what was left of the remains and marked his grave. Then they ventured on to the gold fields, undoubtedly on their best behavior every step of the way.

None of the accounts states the exact location of these atrocities; however, since the aspiring gold seekers had set out from northern Arkansas en route to California, and since the flaying of Mankins is described as taking place soon after they had crossed into Indian territory on the "frontier" or "western plains," the best guess is that they occurred somewhere in what later became Oklahoma.

Lend Me Your Ears

Somebody in Oklahoma was collecting ears. His first victim was found lying in Elk Creek near Hobart, Kiowa County, on March 18, 1907, with a bullet in his head and a piece of railroad iron secured around his neck. The killer had cut off the dead man's nose and one cheek. He also had sliced off both ears and taken them as souvenirs. The body was at first thought to be J. W. Mason, but Mason turned up alive and kicking. The mutilated corpse was never identified.

On July 27, 1907, a well-dressed man with five bullet holes in his chest was found atop a pile of railroad ties in a boxcar at Chickasha, Grady County. He had been killed on the spot rather than transported to the scene, since blood had spattered the ceiling and sides of the car. The murderer had clipped off his ears and carried them away. The victim was carefully embalmed and so well preserved that four years later, in December 1911, a relative identified him as Wesley Yandell of Tribbey.

On August 1, 1907, the earless body of barber Wilbur Gunreth was dumped three miles west of Oklahoma City on the Tenth Street Road. He had been shot four times, his teeth had been battered out, and he had been "otherwise mutilated." This time the killer had left a severed ear on one of the city's main streets.

State and local police were baffled. In October they asked the feds for assistance. But despite the outside help and a reward posted by the governor, the stealer of men's ears was never caught. His identity is known only to the one who determines the weight of the wind and the path of the lightning.

A Stiff Sentence

On November 23, 1906, the police chief of Tahlequah lost his temper when sixteen-year-old William P. teased him. The chief fatally shot William as he tried to run away; then he lost his job and went on trial.

He was convicted of second-degree murder. His attorney appealed, and the ex-chief was released on bail. He went home to await a later trial. For reasons unknown, the court of appeals put off his second trial indefinitely.

On September 17, 1910, an unknown assassin shot him in his yard. That would seem to put an end to the legal wrangle, but on November 16, 1911—more than a year after he had died—the court of criminal appeals affirmed the earlier decision and sentenced the long-deceased man to ten years in prison.

The former chief's mortal shell didn't have to serve the term, of course—*that* would have been silly! But his estate was ordered to pay court costs.

Emma Begs to Differ

On December 21, 1935, Emma W. got into a dispute with her father, Iddis W., at their farmhouse at Eakly. The eighteen-year-old wanted to accompany a neighbor boy to a Christmas party at the schoolhouse. Her father didn't want her to go. Next day, she killed him with a twelve-gauge shotgun as he slept.

She explained her motive to the sheriff: "He was cruel, wouldn't let any of us go anywhere and kept us at home all the time and made us work." Emma had two sisters and two brothers who agreed that Mr. W. would never let them go anywhere but denied that he was violent. The neighbors concurred. Emma, on the other hand, said he "just hit us with whatever he could get ahold of." It was noted that the family didn't seem too broken up over Mr. W.'s untimely end.

The day after the murder, Emma was allowed to attend her father's funeral under guard. She made a strange statement: "I am sorry about it if I am a murderer but I'm not sorry that he's dead." She added, "The only thing I'm afraid of is that they'll sentence me to life or hang me." Emma didn't need to worry about being hanged, at any rate—the instrument of execution in Oklahoma was the electric chair.

When Emma's family realized the full extent of her plight, they abruptly changed their tune: now they claimed to have been abused by Mr. W. for *years*. "He wouldn't let the children go to Sunday school because he thought they liked it," said the widow, Zona. "But now they're going to go every Sunday. I was married . . . nineteen years ago but I don't see how I stood it that long."

Emma went on trial in February 1936. Under oath, she claimed her father had beaten her as though she were livestock, using rocks, sticks, clubs, and chunks of iron as weapons. She made him sound like a villain from a melodrama—"He told me that if I'd do what he wanted, he would be easier on me and the family, and see to it that I got to go places and wouldn't have to work in the fields"—but Mrs. W. corroborated the most outlandish of her daughter's statements.

Emma also said she didn't remember shooting her father.

On February 26, the jury acquitted her on the grounds of insanity. More likely, they were uncomfortable with the thought of sending a teenage girl to the chair. Was she actually insane? It's impossible to determine, but neither she nor the legal system appears to have thought so. Upon her acquittal Emma said, perhaps tellingly and a bit too frankly, "Well, they've declared me crazy. I don't feel any different than I did before they said I was insane, though."

She was sent to the Western Hospital for the Insane at Fort Supply on February 27. Almost exactly a month later she was set free, never to harm another soul as far as the record shows.

An Unseemly Souvenir

Timing is everything, even in the world of crime.

Arthur Gooch kidnapped a pair of police officers in Paris, Texas, and even though he released them he received the death penalty. Americans had been shocked by the recent kidnapping and killing of aviator Charles Lindbergh's infant son; the direct result of this outrage had been the passing of the Lindbergh Law, which made kidnapping a capital offense. Gooch was the first to be sentenced under the new law, and the feds wanted to make an example of him via hanging, a throwback since Oklahoma had adopted the electric chair in 1915.

His mother, Adella, came up with a strange scheme to save him from death row: to finance the traveling she undertook while asking for clemency, she sold tiny souvenir hangman's nooses bearing the slogan "Let's save Arthur Gooch from hanging." Despite her well-intended if borderline tasteless efforts, Gooch was hanged in McAlester, Oklahoma, on June 19, 1936.

Executions among the Choctaw

A writer for the *Buffalo Express* stated in 1895, "Indians as a rule will face death with apparent indifference and seem to have no dread of bullets or bayonets, but all have an unconquerable horror of hanging." For this reason, a law was passed in several states that Indians found guilty of murder should be executed only by shooting. The author of the article got to see this theory put into practical reality when he witnessed the execution of Levi James.

Remarkably, the Choctaw tribe placed so much value on personal honor and bravery that James was allowed to walk free until a few days before his execution date, when he was expected to turn himself in. And so he did; the reporter and his companions met him at the combination Indian courthouse and jail thirty miles from Fort Smith, Arkansas, in what was then called Indian Territory. After a cold, miserable two-day ride in a buckboard, they arrived on December 14, 1883, and found James awaiting the firing squad in his cell, accompanied by his baby, a four-year-old son, and his distraught wife: "He was a full-blood Choctaw, about twenty-five years old, with a fair education. He belonged to one of the best families in his tribe. He had killed another Indian while drunk, and without cause or provocation. His victim belonged to an influential Choctaw family, who had prosecuted the case against James very zealously."

After praying with a missionary, the condemned man—who was handicapped—was led to the woods behind the jail; a blanket was spread on the ground, and James sat down. The "firing squad" consisted of only one elderly Indian with a six-shooter, who had served as an executioner for his people for forty years. "When he stepped out in front of the man to be shot and drew his pistol," the writer reminisced, "the heartbroken wife wept as few Indians ever weep." The children started crying too, as did Levi James at last, leading one to wonder about the stereotype maintaining that Indians are always stoic and reserved. After a while, the sheriff led James's wife and children away. She fled as fast as she could so she would not have to hear the shot that was about to end her husband's life.

Once Mrs. James was out of earshot, the executioner sat on a stump twenty feet from James: "The Sheriff unbuttoned the coat and vest of the condemned man, baring his left breast; then, feeling for the beating of the heart, he pressed his finger for an instant on the spot to give the executioner a mark at which to shoot." The Sheriff held one of James's hands while a deputy held the other.

The lawmen's close proximity to a man seconds away from being shot indicates that they put great store in the executioner's aim. Their faith was justified: "His aim was true. The bullet struck the exact spot indicated by the finger mark. There was a quick jerk, both hands were torn loose from the grip of the officers, and a stream of blood spurted from a ghastly wound." The executioner sat down "as unconcernedly as if he had shot at a tree." A messenger located Mrs. James and told her the worst was over. She returned and embraced Mr. James, staining her dress with blood in the process. Then she left, and Levi's family came to collect him.

The reporter found the old executioner sitting on a rock, puffing away at a pipe, and asked if he always shot condemned men through the heart. The executioner replied, undoubtedly speaking from many years' experience, "No, if you shoot a man through the heart he may live four or five minutes, but shoot through a big blood vessel above the heart and cut it in two, then he will die in a minute."

The reporter remembered another Choctaw execution that had taken place at the end of June 1882: that of Edward Folsom, condemned for murdering a saloonkeeper in August 1881. Like Levi James, he had been given free rein to wander as he pleased until his life was to be ended. The tribe fully expected that he would do the honorable thing and turn himself in at 10:00 a.m. on the day set for his execution.

On the appointed day, at least fifty persons turned up to witness the execution. But by almost 10:00 a.m. the guest of honor had not yet arrived. A white spectator expressed doubt that Folsom would turn up; it seemed to him that no man, white or Indian, would abandon his freedom and voluntarily come to a certain death. One of the condemned man's relatives overheard this and said with indignation, "When a Folsom gives his word he keeps it. You can count on that. He'll be here on time."

At almost that exact moment, Folsom rode up on his horse and announced that he was ready. He chose his cousin to be the executioner. Folsom produced a sheet of paper, tore off a piece, and pinned it to his coat over his heart to serve as a target. The cousin took aim and fired, and two minutes later the world was Folsomless. "He was a murderer," acknowledged the writer, "but his high sense of honor and bravery almost caused that fact to be forgotten."

That He Wasn't

Helena, Oklahoma, July 22, 1912: Young Mr. R., age twenty, hit Mrs. Minnie R. over the head with an iron pipe, then struck her with an ax, then cut her throat with a razor.

Mr. R.'s first name was Meek.

Back to Nature

On December 18, 1891, woodcutters were chopping down an oak in the hills west of Tishomingo. The tree was hollow, with a thin layer of wood that had grown over its entrance. When they felled the oak, it burst open and expelled a human skeleton.

Skeletons are always interesting to find but this one especially so. It had a couple of ribs with bullet wounds, and it sported a leg iron. No one ever figured out who he had been in life, but one attractive theory with explanatory scope and power held that he was an escaped prisoner who had been injured in the ribs after being shot by pursuers, took refuge in a hollow tree, and died in its arboreal embrace. He was never found, and nature took its course, slowly covering the hole in the tree.

A Hard Day at the Office

The Pawnee Bill Wild West Show originated in Oklahoma and traveled around the eastern states at the turn of the last century. One of its more notable performers was a Mexican named George Therma, whose job required him to undergo a hanging sixteen times a week.

Part of the show consisted of a reenactment of a lynching, since those events were so common out West, and easterners were athirst to see one. Therma played the horse thief. The part required him to be lassoed while riding a horse "at breakneck speed," dragged several hundred feet to an artificial tree, and then hanged by a playacting mob.

To prevent getting killed for real, Therma's costume included a stiff lining around the neck of his coat. That didn't help much, however, when his fellow thespians failed to perform their parts correctly. A newspaper account from July 1906 notes, "On several occasions since he has been doing the work the cowboys who hang him have grown careless, and Therma has been cut down more nearly like the dead man he is supposed to be than the live man he wants to be."

One actor wasn't merely sloppy but downright malevolent. Another Mexican named Jose Barraro played the head cowboy, and he thought it a hoot to drag Therma over the roughest terrain he could find before cheering crowds. On one memorable occasion, Barraro pulled Therma over a rock, and the latter spent three weeks in the hospital with a concussion. Therma thought that Barraro had a running wager with the other cowboys that he would kill the imitation horse thief one day.

For all this, Therma was paid $12.50 a week and board or, as his contract put it, "Fifty dollars a month and his cakes." Yet he enjoyed his showbiz career. A reporter noted, "Therma has had his arms broken and a leg dislocated, but he likes the excitement of the job, and while he is occasionally taken from the field to the hospital unconscious, he would not leave the work for anything you could offer him."

Something to keep in mind when the copier jams at work.

3

NIGHTMARISH NEVADA

Bizarre Bequests

Zachary Taylor W. of Reno was ever so proud of his fifteen-foot beard. When he died on December 31, 1926, his will stipulated that his chin carpet be cut off and given to the Whiskerinos Club of Sacramento, a fraternity for similarly hirsute fellows.

In a Pickle

Who hasn't walked around in a cemetery, stared at the ground, and thought, *Hey, what's going on down there?* The answer is very interesting things, sometimes.

For example, Mrs. D. was buried in the Odd Fellows' Cemetery at Paradise in 1879. In 1882, her husband exhumed her body so he could move it to Fort Scott, Kansas. During her time underground, she had gained so much weight from "petrifying" that it took four men to lift her casket. When they peeked inside (who wouldn't?), they found that she looked "as natural as when . . . buried" and that her hair had grown several luxuriant inches. What the folks of the era took to be "petrification" was most likely the accumulation of adipocere, a waxy substance that sometimes forms when a body decomposes under certain conditions. But that doesn't make it any less creepy.

But Who's Counting?

How violent could Wild West towns be? The pioneers who settled Pioche claimed seventy-two men were murdered there before a natural death finally occurred. Historian Lambert Florin claims it was seventy-five, but let's not split hairs; what's a few dead rowdies, more or less? The well-stocked Boot Hill in Pioche—formerly a ghost town, now a tourist spot—is one of its attractions. The dead are subdivided by category; one section includes the mostly unmarked graves of over a hundred murderers.

At the height of its glory days, Pioche had six thousand inhabitants and over seventy saloons. The Nevada state mineralogist visited in 1873 and described the town to the state legislature:

> About one-half of the community are thieves, scoundrels and murderers and then we have some of the best folks in the world, and I don't know but our lives and property are just as safe as with you. You can go uptown and get shot very easily if you choose, or you can live peacefully. I will send you a paper with an account of the last fight. . . . I was in hopes eight or ten would have been killed at least, as these fights are a pest in the community. Peaceful! Sure, peaceful! Sure, if you stayed out of the way of the bullets.

The editor of the local paper expressed similar sentiments: "Some people do not hesitate to fire a pistol or gun at any time, day or night, in this city. Murderers who shoot a man in the back get off scot free but the unfortunate devil who steals a bottle of whiskey or a couple of boxes of cigars has to pay for his small crime."

The *Pioche Daily Record* considered it newsworthy when the town experienced peace for an unprecedented period in summer 1876: "The people of this city have been on their good behavior for nearly two months and there have been no homicides or altercations."

Super Skeletons

In 1911, miners at Lovelock exhumed a number of red-haired mummies in a cave. They ranged in size from over six feet to eight feet tall. Amateur archaeologist John T. Reid contacted the Smithsonian and the anthropology department at the University of Pennsylvania. Neither was interested, but a year later someone from the University of California turned up and showed—to the bafflement of the locals—a singular lack of interest in the potentially important find. Reid's account of the finding of the giants is in the Nevada Historical Society library, and, according to author Jim Brandon, some of the giant bones and artifacts are owned by a private museum in Winnemucca. Giant skeletons turned up in the area sporadically for years afterward: an eight and a half footer was found in February 1931, a ten footer in June of the same year, and one measuring seven feet, seven feet inches in September 1939.

The Trouble with Hairy

Peter S. and John G. were on a hunting expedition in Nevada's Antelope Valley in autumn 1879 when they took a shortcut across a mountain to get back to their ranch. The peak they crossed was inhospitable—it was described, in fact, as "the wildest place in the Antelope range of mountains."

The adventurers were walking around the edge of a chasm when they saw "a huge, hairy object, apparently half man and half beast" running from them at great speed. It mostly resembled a man but had long arms and was as hairy as a gorilla. Thinking it some exotic critter, John fired and hit it in the arm. This only made the creature angry, and instead of running *away* from the hunters he changed course and ran *toward* them.

Peter and John dropped their weapons and ran with a speed and power that might have won them great acclaim and gold medals under other circumstances. They looked behind only when about to drop from exhaustion and were relieved to see that the monster did not pursue them.

William S. claimed that a party of hunters recently had seen the same creature on a mountain fifteen miles from the town of Antelope. There were stories that the "wild man" was actually a lunatic who had escaped to the mountains from California years before. But the reader may recognize in the strange being a passing resemblance to our dear friend Bigfoot.

Poisoned Potable

Here's a legal conundrum: If a person attempting suicide fails to kill himself but takes someone else out by accident, to what degree should he be held responsible under the law? This question was pondered in March 1930 by the *New York Times*, which offered real-life examples as illustrations, including one featuring an unnamed Nevada woman.

She bought strychnine from a drug store and mixed it with whiskey. She claimed later that she had intended to drink it but, unable to work up sufficient nerve, left the deadly concoction out in the open. A man came along—the *Times* did not identify him or explain his relationship to the woman, if any—spied the drink, sniffed it approvingly, and gave in to temptation. He certainly wished he hadn't. Death by strychnine isn't pretty. Symptoms include foaming at the mouth and uncontrollable twitching; the spine stiffens so acutely that the imbiber's back arches like a bow.

In the aftermath, it was suggested that the Nevada woman meant for the dead man to drink the poisoned whiskey all along, and her claim of intended suicide was a subterfuge. The judge ruled that the woman's story about buying the strychnine to end her own existence was true, but she was responsible for second degree murder anyway.

What the Hay?

A young Carson Valley ranch hand named Anderson disappeared without a trace in autumn 1886. An extensive search was undertaken with no results. It was assumed that he had fallen in love with some local girl and run off with her, for love will make us do strange things.

In spring 1887, William Mooney, a Virginia City stable owner, bought bales of alfalfa hay from the ranch where the young man had vanished a few months before. Mooney opened one and found that he had purchased a bonus: the body of Anderson "in a good state of preservation." Belatedly it was remembered that he had last been seen near a hay baler. Putting two and two (i.e., the bale and the body) together, the authorities guessed Anderson had ventured too near the baler in the absence of coworkers, fallen in, gotten baled, and suffocated.

The newly found ranch hand was given a Christian burial, and the hay sold for twenty-five dollars a ton.

Executions

Joseph Behiter killed a Las Vegas showgirl with a pick on July 23, 1931. It was all a silly mistake, as he had intended to kill another woman. He went to the gas chamber in the state prison at Carson City on July 13, 1934. On the way in, he whistled a jolly tune; when he sat in the chair he offered his executioner constructive advice: "Don't strap me to the chair too tightly. It might keep the gas from my lungs."

A Meal That Sticks to Your Ribs

Over a century ago, a hobo in Goldfield was digging around in the trash for something to eat. He found a container of library paste, and evidently thought it akin to bread dough since it contained water and flour. But it also included poisonous alum, and the vagrant died after his ill-advised repast. Today he is buried in Goldfield Pioneer Cemetery under a weathered marker with an inscription that makes tourists do comical double takes: "Unknown Man. Died eating library paste. July 14, 1908."

4

NUMINOUS NORTH DAKOTA

Extraordinary Epitaph

When railroad telegrapher Mathies Braden died in 1882 after falling off of a caboose, his widow erected a tall monument to his memory in Greenwood Cemetery near Bismarck. The wording was most unfortunate: "Stranger call this not / A place of fear and gloom. / To me it is a pleasant spot. / It is my husband's tomb." Braden's widow was German, and it has been conjectured that she wasn't aware of how callous her sentiments sounded when translated into English.

One Murder Attempt Too Many

George M. was suspected of poisoning his wife at the Dewdrop Inn (yes, really!) in London, Ontario, Canada. He went on trial in 1885, was acquitted despite poison having been found in Mrs. M.'s stomach, and removed himself across the border to the Dakota Territory. He got married again too, for the fifth time.

One day in January 1886, the newest Mrs. M. spied her husband putting something in her tea. Rather than make a scene with a direct accusation, she surreptitiously switched cups with him. After all, she *might* be wrong! George downed the tea. During his subsequent death agonies, he admitted that he had tried to murder her. He also confessed that he had poisoned his first four wives in the Ontario cities of Ingersoll and Woodstock.

To Avoid Some Work

On February 9, 1930, all six members of the Albert H. family disappeared from their farmhouse a mile north of Schafer. While everyone in the vicinity scratched their heads over that one, the family's twenty-two-year-old hired hand, Charles B., moved into the house. He said the former owners had just abruptly decided to move away. Soon Charles's father, James, joined him.

Neighbors got suspicious in October, when Charles and James sold the H. family's livestock and crops. In November 1930 James B. also vanished, and heads were treated to a new round of scratching. He wasn't dead, though; he sent his son a letter from Lake Oswego, Oregon, on December 2.

Police arrested Charles and asked him on what authority he had sold the property. On December 11, under questioning, Charles revealed where four members of the H. family and parts of a fifth could be discovered. The police dug and found the battered bodies in the suggested spot. Only Mrs. H. remained missing.

Asked to explain these extraordinary circumstances, Charles told a suitably weird and farfetched tale. He said that Mrs. H. had gone insane and killed her family with a hammer. Had Charles disarmed her? Called the cops? Run away? No. Evidently, in the spirit of neighborliness, he had helped her bury her bludgeoned dead, after which she had taken flight, leaving Charles and his father to live in the house for several months although they knew the bodies of five murder victims were enriching the property's soil.

No one believed Charles's tale (for some reason), and after a minister and his mother pleaded with him to tell the truth, he did:

On that day last February, Charles had shot nineteen-year-old Daniel H. in the barn following an argument over chores. Sixteen-year-old Leland H. had come to investigate, and Charles had shot him too after a brand-new quarrel.

When Mr. and Mrs. H. had come to the barn to check on the whereabouts of their sons, Charles had shot them as well, perhaps to avoid yet another dispute. Realizing he couldn't reverse his course now, Charles killed a three-year-old and clubbed the family's three-month-old baby. Charles bludgeoned each body to be certain they were dead, then buried them all in the barn.

That was okay for a while, but then the bodies of Mrs. H. and the three-year-old became conspicuous by their decomposition. Charles B.— who had committed six murders to *avoid* chores—performed the arduous chore of exhuming the two most odiferous corpses and stashing them away in a cave.

Charles vowed he was the only guilty party, but suspicious lawmen arrested his father in Toledo, Oregon, on December 13 and brought him back to North Dakota.

On January 29, 1931, a lynch mob yanked Charles B. out of his cell and hanged him from the new Cherry Creek Bridge. It was North Dakota's last lynching. On June 18, James was found guilty of first degree murder and sent to prison for life.

A Hasty Trial, and with Good Reason

Turtle Lake is a small community north of Bismarck. It was founded in 1905 and thus had barely existed when what is likely to forever remain its most notorious murder case occurred on a farm a few miles from town.

On April 24, 1920, John Kraft wondered why the Wolf family's laundry was hanging outside in rainy weather. Investigating, he found the less-than-pristine bodies of the entire household: Russian immigrant and farmer Jacob Wolf and his daughters, Edna, age eight, and Maria, age ten, had been shotgunned in the barn and partially covered with hay.

The cellar contained four more—Mrs. Beatta Wolf and the other daughters: Bertha, thirteen; Lydia, six; and Martha, three. Adding to this profusion was the corpse of the hired boy, thirteen-year-old Jacob Hofer. The killer seemed to have just barely enough of a heart to spare the nine-month-old baby, Emma, found alive but hungry in her cradle beside an open window.

A mass funeral was held at the farm and drew a crowd estimated at 2,500. The seven Wolfs and their hired boy are buried side by side in a long line in Turtle Lake Cemetery. (Nearby is the gravestone of the family's sole survivor, Emma Wolf Hanson, who died in 2003.)

It was estimated that the massacre had occurred on April 22. Wolf had been well-to-do but so indiscreet as to tell several acquaintances that he kept a large sum of money in a safe at home. At first detectives thought robbery was the motive, but the cache was untouched, and the murders didn't seem the work of a professional killer—i.e., a burglar—since clues were scattered about with a profligate richness. For example, shotgun shells were everywhere, and the cellar yielded a bloody hatchet. The killer generously left his bloody overalls behind in the kitchen. A swamp located a mile north of the Wolf farm seemed a jim-dandy place to hide evidence; it was searched, and up came a double-barreled twelve-gauge shotgun. It would have been hard to miss since the weapon's stock, apparently removed by the killer, was floating on the water. The killer also helpfully provided footprints that showed where he had trudged in the mud to the edge of the swamp and thrown in the gun. And the fact that there was only one set of tracks suggested a lone perpetrator, not several.

The sheriff became especially suspicious of one of the murdered family's neighbors, farmer Henry Layer, who showed up during the investigation and ostentatiously complained about how Mr. Wolf's dog had been menacing his livestock. His manner seemed so odd that he was arrested on May 11 and taken in for questioning. He folded like a deck chair and confessed the next day.

So what was Layer's motive for shooting and hacking two adults and six children? Greed, perhaps? Jealousy? Deviant sexual impulses? Temporary insanity? Nah. Layer was just mad because Wolf's dog had bitten one of his cows, and he thought exterminating the family was the proper way to seek redress. He admitted he hadn't killed the baby only because he hadn't known she was there.

Layer was tried at a supersonic pace, probably to save him from a lynching. He was found guilty on May 13, the day after his confession, and sentenced to life in prison. He was fortunate indeed not to get the death penalty, considering the brutality of his crime and the trivial reason for committing it. Nevertheless, Layer got lucky twice—depending on one's definition of "luck"—in that his life sentence lasted only five years. He died in prison on March 21, 1925, of heart trouble following an operation for appendicitis.

Sure, Why Not?

L. S. Elmer was Sheriff Miller's deputy; he also boarded with Miller in Wahpeton. In the same house resided Mollie Kerbell, a young woman from Bohemia and the sheriff's employee.

On July 25, 1888, Deputy Elmer asked Mollie if she had plans for going out that evening, a question that implies he was sweet on her. She answered sarcastically that she would come and go as she pleased, an answer that implies she did not reciprocate the affection.

The riposte did not sit well with Elmer, who impulsively shot her dead on the spot. Perhaps some citizens were surprised by this sordid turn of events, but Elmer may have been the most surprised person of all, as he said afterward that he had no idea why he'd done it.

Mollie's body lay in state in the courtroom on July 26, and thousands removed their hats and trooped through to gaze at her. The local Bohemian population swore vengeance.

That night, a mob pounded on Sheriff Miller's door, in search of Elmer. The lawman put up no resistance, later offering a novel explanation: he had recognized several of the lynchers as personal buddies, and "the life of the murderer was not worth the life of a friend." The fact that he was outnumbered ninety-nine to one might also have had something to do with his decision. The record does not state what Deputy Elmer thought of Sheriff Miller's low opinion of his worth.

With the sheriff's tacit permission, the mob removed the deputy from his cell and hanged him from a bridge over the Bois de Sioux River. Hundreds of people witnessed the lynching, including women, and the press assures us that all "went home satisfied."

A Dubious Verdict

For some time McLean County had been overrun with horse thieves, and the farmers were darn sick of it. So when one of the leading members of that despised profession, James O'Neil, was captured on June 22, 1884, his victims knew just what to do. They hanged him from a telegraph pole, using the most convenient (and ironic) rope available: the same lariat he had used to steal horses.

The coroner's jury soberly examined O'Neil's body on June 23 and issued a classic verdict that implied rather strongly that they had no interest in bringing the lynchers to justice: "The deceased met his death by suicide, riding his horse to the telegraph pole, tying the rope to his neck and the pole, and letting his horse go from under him."

Making Their Job Easy

The wife of a Mandan ex-mayor was living on a claim near Minnewaukan in December 1884 when she overheard a very disturbing conversation between her husband and son-in-law, who were making plans to murder her.

Did Mrs. H. call the cops, go into hiding, or kill the plotters first? No, she made her would-be murderers' job easy by taking the task out of their hands. She ran with her baby three miles to a neighbor's house, after which she slashed her throat with a butcher knife while gazing in the mirror.

She survived long enough to explain the circumstances, and then the usual lynch mob set out for her husband and son-in-law.

Snowbound

The Great Northern train was due to arrive in St. Paul on March 28, 1902. It didn't get there. The reason was unknown for several days, since its passengers were cut off from the rest of the world.

On March 27, the train had left Williston, North Dakota, just in time to encounter what was later called the worst blizzard the region had experienced in years. The engineer had hoped to make it to Minot, but near the town of Ray the snow was so deep the locomotive could go no farther.

The situation was as critical as a critical situation could be. The engineer had an idea: perhaps he could separate the engine from the boxcars and drive it back to Williston for help. He uncoupled the engine and left the passenger cars on the side tracks. He and the conductor left with haste, but the engine was caught in a snowdrift a short distance away, and they had to abandon the rescue effort.

Meanwhile, eight passenger cars containing 250 souls were snowbound on the tracks as the drifts grew ever deeper. There was no way to communicate their plight, no heat source, and enough food for only two small meals per person a day.

Women huddled under blankets, and men wore their overalls day and night. Second-class passengers demanded that they get as much food as the first-class travelers and balked when told women and children should have first crack at the rations.

On March 31, F. W. Colegrove, professor of philosophy at the University of Washington—facing despondency, cabin fever, unremitting cold, and the very real possibility of starvation—slashed his throat with a razor. He did not die, but one wonders whether his gaunt companions mentally counted his calories.

Finally, the passengers broke into the conductor's box and found a telegraph. *Very* fortunately for them, an electrician just happened to be on board. He left the relative safety of the train and tapped the wire of a telegraph pole, the early twentieth century equivalent of hacking a computer. He told operators at Minot and Williston about the stranded train.

A snowplow from Minot made it to the train after an all-night slog, very dangerous since the blizzard was not over. The plow operator brought a surgeon, who took care of the wounded professor. After their ordeal, which had lasted for four days and five nights, the passengers were rescued, probably with a lifelong urge to punch in the nose anyone who recited the then-popular poem "The Beautiful Snow."

5

SPOOKY SOUTH DAKOTA

Encore

Anyone can slash his own throat from ear to ear; farm laborer William K. did so with a six-inch pocket knife at Sioux Falls on December 22, 1934. But William added a little something extra to the usual routine by swallowing the knife when he was finished. He expired the next day.

Murdering a Monstrosity

The pride of Archie B.'s traveling tent show was a creature that seemed somewhat simian yet somewhat human, and for this reason the showman advertised it as "The Missing Link." Whatever it was, it did not get along with Archie, and they had a fight in July 1899 while doing a show in Bonesteel. Archie walloped his "What Is It" over the ear with a club. It died and Archie was arrested for murder.

His attorneys ingeniously argued that no one knew if the creature was human—and if it wasn't, their client could not be charged with murder. It was left to the court to determine whether the freak belonged to the human family or otherwise, and if the lack of follow-up stories in the national press is any indication, they were unable to decide.

You're a Bad Man, Charlie Brown

Charles Brown worked as a cook for Col. L. P. Stone and his wife, Emma. In early May 1897, he was fired for being drunk on the job and threatening his employers. On May 14, while pilfering his former bosses' restaurant for valuables, Charles panicked and nearly decapitated Emma with a handy meat cleaver. He also strangled the family's watchdog before he split the scene. A waitress found these horrors in the storeroom.

It did not take the law long to figure out the killer's identity, and Charles was summarily arrested. There was no substantial evidence in his favor. At his trial, the defense lawyers performed the legal equivalent of shrugging their shoulders by saying, "Your honor and gentlemen of the jury, the defense in this case has no evidence to offer. Soon after being appointed by this court to defend the accused the true nature of the case came to us so forcibly that we have no theories of a defense, but allow the case to be submitted upon the evidence adduced by the prosecution. The defense rests."

It took the jury a paltry twenty minutes to find Charles guilty and recommend a death sentence. At last he broke down and admitted his guilt, which had never been in doubt for a moment anyway.

But there was one wrinkle that made Charles's execution unique: when the end came for the repentant cook, the colonel asked—and received—permission from the sheriff to be the official hangman. The final event occurred at Deadwood on July 14, two months to the day after the murder.

Consolation Prize

The animosity between cattle ranchers and sheepherders in the Old West was legendary, so when shepherd John E. was murdered in Fall River County in August 1898, it was no surprise that cattlemen were arrested. What *was* surprising was their sheer number: thirty-two! They admitted shooting John but claimed it had been self-defense. The cattlemen went on trial at Hot Springs at the end of the year, and all were acquitted the week before Christmas.

But to show their hearts were in the right place, they rode to the dead man's cabin on December 26 and knocked on the door. When the widow answered, the delegation's leader delivered this oration: "We have come to make you a little Christmas present. We shot your husband, but it was in self-defense. We know you are without funds. We would gladly restore your husband, but that is impossible, so we do the next best thing—give you the means to support yourself and children. If you need more, call on us."

The cattlemen handed her a bag containing one hundred dollars in gold, doffed their hats, and rode away. One newspaper commented, perhaps sarcastically: "If, now, any of the cattlemen happens to be a single man and is willing to marry the widow, their record will be unexceptionable. It is so seldom that the slayers of men do the handsome thing that this case deserves special mention."

A Community's Revenge

George C. lived in Terry, a mining community near Deadwood. He was not one of the more upstanding citizens, since he beat his wife in public, a very foolish move in a town that had a low tolerance for such behavior. He was arrested and placed in jail in August 1908.

Along came a lynch mob that set him free, but only so they could force him to run a gauntlet of miners wielding blacksnake whips. The mob intended to kill him, but, interestingly, the town's women encouraged them to spare his life and merely banish him.

What was the outcome? Unfortunately, the old newspapers do not tell us.

Interrupted by the Phone

At 2:00 a.m. on April 16, 1885, a mob removed murderer James H. Bell of Harrold from his jail cell and, lacking a sense of irony, carried him away to hang him from the flagstaff of the Pierre courthouse.

As they prepared to take the law into their own hands, the mob heard a telephone ringing nearby. The sound was disturbing, and they acted in such haste that they didn't bother to tie their victim's arms. The sheriff arrived and cut down Bell's body as the mob scattered. Much to everyone's surprise he was still alive, but he died shortly after the rescue.

At least the lynchers left alone Bell's accomplice, Mr. Bennett, who had confessed. They must have considered hanging him, however, since they had arrived with two ropes.

Five Mummies

William Allen was prospecting near Buffalo Gap in the Badlands in February 1887. As he sank a shaft, the earth crumbled beneath him, and his tools disappeared down a newly made hole. Luckily for Allen, he was tied to a rope attached to a windlass and climbed his way out. Wondering what could possibly be down in the hole—and no doubt hoping it was something valuable—he got a longer rope and lowered himself down.

After descending eighty feet, he landed in a cavern twenty feet square. But instead of gold, he found this: "He was horrified to see huddled in one corner the bodies of five persons—a man, a woman, and three children.

They were shriveled to less than half the size of human beings, the dried-up flesh giving them the appearance of mummies. The hair was still on their heads and the fingernails were perfect but very long. On the side of the cave were some strange hieroglyphics and marks as though the inmates had tried to dig themselves out; and, failing in this, left the story of their fate."

Allen theorized that the remains were of a family trapped by a landslide, possibly hundreds of years before.

6

UNUSUAL UTAH

Premature Burial

On June 20, 1874, a youth named William L. attended a picnic at Salt Lake City. After an invigorating dip in the lake, he exercised further by fooling around on a swing. While so doing, he slumped to the ground in a dead faint. His fellow picnickers failed to revive him and took him home in a carriage. The doctor plied his trade to no effect and reluctantly pronounced William dead on June 21—reluctantly because the patient didn't seem so very dead after all. Despite being unresponsive to stimuli, he had a "singularly lifelike appearance." William's nervous friends delayed the funeral by a couple of days just in case.

June 22 came and went with no signs of life. The doctors stated confidently that he died of heart disease, so the interment took place on June 23. A neighbor who attended the funeral warned that William was not dead but in a coma—and he spoke from experience, having once slipped into a deathlike state of suspended animation for eight days.

A couple of William's cronies were far from satisfied and launched a whispering campaign holding that the young man had been buried before his time. The rumors provoked a full-blown citywide sense of great unease. William's friends received permission to open the grave merely to satisfy their curiosity, since nothing could be done to help William at that point anyway. On July 9 the grave was spaded, the coffin unearthed, and the lid opened. What happened next is best left to the eloquence of a reporter: "The body was turned over on its side. The skin and great pieces of flesh had been torn from the face, the hair pulled out in huge patches from the scalp, the grave clothes and coffin lining torn in shreds, and the fingernails worn down to the quick by the frantic efforts of the man to burst the cerements of his grave. The sight was the most terrible ever witnessed, and the stoutest-hearted of the party nearly fainted when the lid of the coffin was removed."

There wasn't much the doctors could say other than a heartfelt "oops."

In a Pickle

Two boys, Hal O. and Gene L., were playing in the hills two miles from Ephraim on August 4, 1934, when they saw the corner of a box poking up from the ground. They unearthed it, perhaps thinking it contained treasure. Instead, the rotten box held the well-preserved body of a two-year-old boy. The sheriff took the remains to a taxidermist, who agreed that whoever had done the job had performed it expertly.

The whole thing was a mystery. There were no reports of missing children in the area. How long had the child been dead? Because of the preservation, it was impossible to tell. If the child had been murdered, why bother preserving him in the first place? If he had died of natural causes, why embalm him at home and bury him secretly? These profound questions evidently were never answered to anyone's satisfaction.

Your Typical French Grave-Robbing Hermit

Jean Baptiste was one of the most unpleasant citizens in Utah's history. He was a French immigrant, and for over thirty years he lived the life of an unfriendly—and naked—hermit at Church Island (now Antelope Island) in the southeast sector of Great Salt Lake.

Baptiste first moved to Salt Lake City in the 1850s, joined the Mormons, and was appointed cemetery sexton. He made extra income collecting junk and secondhand clothing, which he sold to Jewish merchants. Baptiste's besetting sins were greed and miserliness, and he gained a reputation for packing his cabin with boxes and barrels of scavenged items and dressing like a vagabond.

Heads turned and eyebrows rose one day in 1862 when formerly ragged Baptiste strutted around in a splendid suit—especially since the suit looked like the one a wealthy visitor to the city had been buried in a few days before. An exhumation was ordered, and the stranger proved to be as naked in death as he had been at birth. A committee examined the barrels in Baptiste's cabin and found the grave clothes of over two hundred persons—men, women, and children, mostly Mormons buried in the cemetery where the Frenchman served as sexton.

The ghoul was captured and jailed after barely escaping a lynching. Brigham Young ordered that these words be impressed on Baptiste's forehead with a hot iron: "Branded for Robbing the Dead." Then Baptiste was taken by canoe to Church Island, without clothing, food, or provisions, to be banished for life. He had to make his living as best he could. He didn't dare leave the island for fear of being mobbed.

He was still living there, nude and incoherent, as late as 1895. Occasionally swimmers and boaters would be lost on Salt Lake and their bodies never found; rumor held that if they washed ashore at Church Island, Baptiste converted their bodies into quick and easy meals, but no one was brave enough to confirm it. Mormons and Indians alike warned newcomers to avoid the island at all costs. Hunters and explorers who did venture near the "human monster" stated that he lived in a cave that housed human remains and pieces of boats that had washed ashore. He drank water that dripped from the crags and subsisted mainly on gulls and pelicans. Those who had the pleasure of seeing Baptiste described him as "old, stooping, destitute of clothing, incapable of speech, and covered with long hair. Upon the appearance of man he utters a wild, weird shriek and rushes to the cavern from which he cannot be enticed or forced to return."

Workers United

On June 1, 1910, a premature powder explosion blew to particles twenty-four Italian and Greek laborers and their foreman, Hugh M., at a quarry at Devil's Slide. The bodies were so mangled it was impossible to identify them individually. The foreman's mother attempted to identify him but could not. She requested that the Morgan County authorities give her permission to bury all twenty-five men together in Hugh's grave in Calvary Cemetery in Salt Lake City.

Her request was granted, and the mixed fragments were given as dignified a burial as possible on February 18, 1911. The reason for the long delay is uncertain.

Cult Followings

The Home of Truth cult was originally centered near Blanding. One of their members, Mrs. Edith P., died early in 1935, but the others refused to bury her, convinced that she would return to life after they performed certain rituals including force-feeding her corpse and bathing her daily in salt water to maintain freshness. She was stored in a cabin at Photograph

Gap and zealously guarded by cult members. No outsiders were permitted to take a peep.

In June the state's health department found out about the unburied dead woman and sent an inspector. He talked his way into Edith's cabin and found her partially mummified from the daily saline soaking.

On November 22—nine months after Edith's death—cult leader Marie O. said, "The recreation will be soon now." The health department, skeptical that a long-dead woman could be restored to existence, got a court order to ascertain whether Edith had yet become a public health menace. Court order notwithstanding, the Home of Truth curtly denied their request.

In October 1936—after the passage of almost *another* year—Marie grudgingly admitted that Edith was not among the living. But there was cause for optimism. Marie declared, "We are few, but hundreds are watching us for an indication we are on the right track. Suppose people do laugh—they laughed at Noah, too!" True, but on the other hand, people also laughed at the Three Stooges.

"We are making satisfactory progress," added Marie, "but the time is not ripe for details."

The Utah Health Department continued to be concerned not with the ripeness of the details but rather with the ripeness of Edith. Had she at last commenced decomposing? The Home of Truth members would not allow the department to enter their compound. (By this point the cult had moved from Blanding to near Monticello.) Then Edith disappeared, according to the few in the know who were willing to talk, and the authorities accused the cultists of hiding her.

In April 1937—after another half year had passed—the state health commissioner got tired of playing nice and demanded that the cult cough up a death certificate. Marie O. obstinately refused to sign such a document on the grounds that Edith wasn't really dead and would be fully animated again very soon. She said, "I am in communication with [Edith]. We not only expect her to be restored to us in physical life, but we expect her to be recognized by others." When the cultists were asked whether the missing body had been cremated or buried, they would say only that it had "dematerialized."

On April 29, the state health commissioner sent the director of the State Public Health Laboratory to reason with the Home of Truth colonists. The director must have been persuasive because the state of Utah finally emerged triumphant. A death certificate was filed for Edith P. long after the fact of her demise—she had officially died in San Juan County on February 11, 1935, age fifty-eight.

But what had happened to the body? It came out that the corpse had not been kept aboveground nearly as long as the health authorities had believed. A former cultist, Thomas R., said that he had cremated it in August 1935 on Marie O.'s secret instructions. The dead woman's husband, Elmer, had been purposely kept in the dark. "I doubt if Elmer P. will believe anything except what Marie tells him," mused Thomas. "[He] does not consider himself a widower and is looking forward to his wife's return." Mr. P. must have confronted reality eventually because there is a monument to Edith in Morris Hill Cemetery in Boise, Idaho.

A Dupe Murders a Cad

It looked bad enough when Utah's former senator, sixty-three-year-old Arthur Brown, was shot through his bladder in Washington, DC, on December 8, 1906. It looked even worse when it was known that the shooter was Mrs. Anna M. Bradley, a thirty-four-year-old divorced woman from Salt Lake City. But the fact that the shooting had occurred in Brown's room at the Raleigh Hotel *really* set eyebrows rising and tongues wagging. As a modern politician might say, it made for bad optics.

Mrs. Bradley was escorted to a jail cell, where she received telegrams from friends back in Utah offering assistance. "Everything will come out all right," she said confidently. "Senator Brown will recover and I will never be placed on trial." From his hospital bed, the feverish Brown declared that he would recover. Bradley and Brown were both wrong.

The district attorney visited Brown to get a statement in case he should die, but Brown refused to speak. Both the ex-senator and his shooter were notably, one might even say suspiciously, reluctant to discuss the reason for their little disagreement.

In contrast to Mrs. Bradley, who received many offers of help from gentlemen, nobody offered Brown much assistance. Soon he was beyond all aid anyway. He lingered until December 12; even in his final minutes he refused to divulge why he was shot.

The law was determined to find the cause, of course, and Mrs. Bradley was held on a charge of murder. She refused to pose for an official police mug shot. Amazingly, the authorities acquiesced, which suggests that even this early in the investigation she was treated with more gallantry than would have been given to, say, Three-Fingers Louie the Brooklyn Moiderer. No doubt Mrs. Bradley would have preferred that the police drop the investigation into her past as well, but they were not willing to extend courtesy to a lady *that* far, and the ensuing revelations provided months of titillation for newspaper readers coast to coast.

For starters, the late Arthur Brown was unmasked as a major cad. Originally from southern Michigan, Brown had become a noted attorney in Kalamazoo. His first marriage had ended when he'd taken up with a mistress, Isabelle Cameron. He went so far as to buy a house, a team of horses, and a carriage for her although his friends warned him that it was disgraceful. One night Mrs. Brown found Isabelle in her husband's office and tried to shoot her. To escape these scandals, Arthur Brown moved to Salt Lake City in 1876. Soon afterward, Isabelle Cameron also moved to the city, and their fling continued.

Brown proved to be as successful a lawyer in Utah as he had been in Michigan, and his practice flourished despite his mistress living openly with him. The shame was lessened somewhat when he divorced his wife and married Isabelle a few months later.

Somehow all of these misdeeds did no harm to Brown's rising career in politics, and he served as Utah's senator from 1896 to 1897. Arthur and Isabelle attended the Republican National Convention at St. Louis in 1896, where she introduced him to Anna Bradley. Big mistake! Before long Mr. Brown had a new mistress.

Mrs. Bradley—separated from her husband, who lived in Nevada—gave birth to a son in 1900, whom she named Arthur Brown Bradley. Isabelle Brown, who appears to have been a bit slow on the uptake, evidently did not find this suspicious.

Mr. Brown cut out for Los Angeles. A few weeks later, Mrs. Bradley moved there too. This was too much for Isabelle, who started having misgivings about her husband's fidelity. She discovered that he kept a secret apartment on Second South Street in Salt Lake City for convenient assignations when he happened to be home. She forced her way in and found many love letters written by her friend Mrs. Bradley. They were written in code, but Mrs. Brown found a sheet containing the key. Her fury grew as she deciphered two bushels' worth of letters.

Next, Isabelle Brown did something that aficionados of the art of petty revenge will admire. She sent a collect message by wire to her husband in Los Angeles, a missive so long that it cost him ten dollars (almost $250 in modern currency!) to get it. It was "filled with the keenest satire and invective," according to a news account, and Brown must have known he was in big trouble since she wrote it in his own secret lovers' code. That wasn't all: she had her husband and her former friend arrested for adultery. Charges were later dropped, but Isabelle sued him and got $150 a month (over $3,500 in modern currency) as temporary alimony pending their divorce—which never occurred.

As a legal compromise, it was agreed that Arthur Brown would stay in California and have nothing more to do with either woman. Instead he moved to Pocatello, Idaho, soon to be joined by Mrs. Bradley. Mrs. Brown caught wind of it, traveled to Pocatello, and confronted the lovers in a hotel room with her lawyer in tow. "The scene that followed beggars description," said a reporter. In essence, Mrs. Brown tried twice to kill Mrs. Bradley and was stopped only by the strong arm of her attorney. Arthur pointed out that Isabelle had stolen him away from his first wife back in Kalamazoo and therefore was on no moral high ground, an argument that naturally did nothing to calm the situation. The episode ended with Mrs. Brown saying she never wanted to see either her husband or her so-called friend ever again. She angrily returned to the Brown residence on East South Temple Street in Salt Lake City.

A few months later the ex-senator, finding it impossible to leave well enough alone, moved back to Salt Lake City. He was wise enough not to return to his wife and old house, however, and took up residence at the Independence Hotel. A week later Mrs. Bradley, still finding Mr. Brown irresistible, turned up as well.

Mrs. Brown hired detectives to follow the adulterous couple, who were caught in Brown's hotel apartment in fall 1902. In court Mrs. Bradley pled guilty, was released on her own recognizance, and was never charged. Brown, on the other hand, pled not guilty and was acquitted by the jury. Their verdict seemed pointless in retrospect when, shortly after the trial, Mrs. Bradley gave birth to a second illegitimate son; Brown admitted to friends that the child was his.

The real-life soap opera was far from over. Later the two women got into a fight in Brown's office—why, one can't help wondering, did they think him such a catch worth battling over? The wife was equipped with a lasso; she tied it around the mistress and beat her with the free end. Senator Brown did not interfere.

Somehow, some way, Mrs. Brown lured her wayward husband to return to the domestic circle. He moved back in with her, but the reconciliation lasted only six months. Isabelle Brown died of cancer in August 1905.

The lovers were free to reunite, and "reunite" they did—very often, it appears. Brown proposed marriage to Mrs. Bradley, knowing full well she couldn't accept since she was still married to her Nevada husband. After she went through the trouble of getting a divorce, she requested that the former senator keep his promise. But now that the path to matrimony was clear, Brown refused to marry her, offering one weak excuse after another.

All of which is prelude to the fatal events of December 1906. One might think the unpleasant and very public encounters between his second wife and his mistress would have convinced Mr. Brown to take up a different hobby. However, the lesson was lost on him. He also did not learn the folly of keeping incriminating letters around. When Mrs. Bradley forced her way into Brown's Washington hotel room, she found letters written to Brown by Anna C. Adams, mother of actress Maude Adams and described as "a friend of the family." She appears to have been more than just a friend. The letters' contents were not revealed, but since they were in Mrs. Bradley's possession when she was arrested, one may assume that whatever was in them led her to shoot Brown. She didn't need to crack a secret code to read them, either.

The inquest regarding the former senator's murder was held on December 13. Mrs. Bradley was the very embodiment of unconcern; she must have thought the whole thing a minor inconvenience and that she'd be dismissed right away. Instead, the jury decided that her case would have to come to trial. She gave everyone the spectacle they fully expected by ostentatiously keeling over in a dead faint, then was led back to her cell.

The nation's press could not decide which character was sleazier, Mr. Brown or Mrs. Bradley. Concerning Brown, the editorialist at the *Louisville Courier-Journal* implied that he richly deserved his fate: "A man so unmindful of domestic obligations, so lacking in high moral sensibilities, and so utterly blind to the beauty of pure love as was former Senator Brown of Utah, is apt to meet with such a death as came to him. . . . Brown's grossness seemed to have no saving grace. He was false to his home, to his family, and to himself. He was totally oblivious, apparently, to the meaning of righteousness and to the glory of goodness."

The editorial ended with a zinger: "He was just an all-around bad man, and he died a bad man's death." But at least his funeral in Salt Lake City was attended by nine hundred persons, including "the most prominent attorneys in the state."

People who considered Arthur Brown a consummate villain received more grist for their mills when the contents of his will were divulged, which one commentator described as "post-mortem revenge. . . . Had [Brown] foreseen his death at the hands of Mrs. Bradley he could have devised no more ingenious revenge." In this spiteful legal document, dated August 24, 1906, four months before his murder, Brown offered his longstanding mistress some digital disrespect, if I may coin a euphemism. He declared that neither of her illegitimate children were his, and he didn't intend to leave them anything even if they were:

I do not devise or give or bequeath anything to any of the children of Mrs. Anna M. Bradley. I do not think either or any child born to Mrs. Anna M. Bradley is or are mine, but whether such child or children is or not, I expressly provide that neither or any of them shall receive anything of my estate. I never married Anna M. Bradley and never intend to. If she should pretend that any such relation ever existed between us to justify such inference I direct my executors to contest any claims of any kind she may present, and I direct that she receive nothing from my estate.

And his estate was considerable, too—approximately $70,000 (modern equivalent: nearly $1.5 million), all of which went to his two legitimate offspring by his two wives. Mrs. Bradley was not about to meekly accept the terms of the will, as we shall see. But that had to wait. First item of business for her was to avoid going to prison for murder.

She finally went to trial in DC in November 1907, almost a year after her dark deed. Plenty of chivalrous men in those days had qualms about seeing a woman prosecuted to the full extent of the law, no matter what she might have done, and Mrs. Bradley had more than her share of defenders. The prosecution was worried that her legal team might resort to the "unwritten law." This notion was based on the concept—not codified in any law books, hence its name—that some acts of murder and mayhem were justified by extenuating circumstances. For example, it was often successfully argued in court that a man or woman had a right to kill anyone who broke up the sanctity of their home by seducing their spouse; women were considered warranted if they clobbered someone who spread rumors denigrating their character; and in many cases, women were acquitted for murdering rascals who seduced them after promising marriage and then didn't follow through. The Brown murder certainly fit the last category.

While modern feminists revile the days when women could not serve on juries, ironically this very circumstance often worked in the favor of women on trial, due to the sentimentality and squeamishness of male jurors, who saw themselves as protectors and would jump through logical hoops to ensure that female defendants got off with the lightest punishments possible—or none at all. To give these jurors plenty of opportunities for rationalization, Anna Bradley's attorneys offered a plea of insanity. *Temporary* insanity, of course, because she was in her right mind now. If necessary, they could also argue the unwritten law. (Spoiler alert: this threadbare tactic proved unnecessary.)

It took a while to compose a jury because so many potential jurors said they were opposed to capital punishment *for women* (note emphasis;

presumably, they'd have had no problem sending a rogue of their own gender straight to his Maker).

When the trial began on November 14, the first important witness was the manager of the hotel where Brown had been shot. He said the mortally injured man "had told him that Mrs. Bradley did the shooting and that she had given him trouble all his life." It will be observed that Brown had somehow forgotten to tell the manager that he'd had an equal share in bringing this trouble upon himself.

The prosecution intended to show that the killing had been premeditated. They presented police officers to whom Anna had admitted that she'd done it on purpose. A witness from Salt Lake City said that six months before the murder, Anna had confided that if Brown didn't marry her and make their children legitimate, she would kill him.

Anna's lawyer argued that Arthur Brown had so dominated her that she'd felt she had no choice but to resort to murder. The defense would show that Mr. Brown had "performed more than one criminal act on her with his own hands [that is, abortions—their proof was simply taking her word for it] and that he had presented her with the pistol with which she killed him, telling her that she should use it on his wife if she gave her trouble."

Oh, also, there was a strain of insanity in Mrs. Bradley's family. When Anna took the stand on November 18, she made a point of looking as "frail and weak" as possible. She sat still, with her face buried in her hands, for an entire hour. Reporters who had seen her just after the shooting stated under oath that she had seemed "agitated" and looked "wild and haggard." Doctors who had known her before the murder said her physical condition "was likely to produce mental aberration or at least irresponsibility for her actions." Anna's mother talked about the time her daughter had gotten whacked in the head with a hoe as a child and had bad headaches afterward. On such lame evidence as this—but *of course* she seemed agitated and wild just after shooting someone!—Bradley's lawyers attempted to prove temporary insanity.

Perhaps figuring that yanking the heartstrings might work better, on November 19 Mrs. Bradley played on the jurors' sympathy by telling the whole sordid tale of her relations with Mr. Brown. The tale of her shame was full of pathos and tears and heartbreak and the cynical ex-senator's broken promises. He had intimidated her; she had sacrificed her health for him; she had thought about suicide once. But there had been good moments too, she said, like when he'd written her up to five letters a day and they'd read poetry together (plenty of winsome smiles to the jury while relating this part).

By the time she was finished, there wasn't a dry eye among the jury.

Mrs. Bradley returned to the stand the next day. This time she had to face skeptical cross-examination, which proved far less to her liking than telling woeful stories. What, the prosecution wanted to know, had she been doing following Brown to Washington, DC, in the first place? Had this not indicated premeditation? No, she explained; she had felt that if she'd visited him somewhere away from Salt Lake City, in a place where there was no "local influence," he might finally keep his vows to marry her. When she arrived at his hotel room he was out, and while waiting for him she happened to notice a letter to him written by Anna C. Adams, the actress's mother, and she couldn't resist reading it. She was overcome with jealousy and disappointment after reading its contents. (Some have speculated that Brown proposed marriage to Mrs. Adams instead.) Then he returned to the room, and they argued, and as for shooting him—well, she must have a mental block because she didn't remember that at all.

Her defense team produced an interesting document on November 21, in which Brown admitted that he had sired two illegitimate sons by Anna Bradley. (Remember that he denied it in his mean-spirited will.) The note was dated February 10, 1905, and was presented by Col. Maurice Kaighn, a Salt Lake City attorney who had been a friend of Brown's for thirty years. Kaighn said Mrs. Bradley had brought the document to his office when the ink was still wet and that she had practically danced with joy, figuring that the dilatory Brown would finally fulfill his longstanding promise and marry her. She had figured wrongly, of course, but the document proved invaluable to her case: at last there was evidence other than her word that the ex-senator was the father of her children, in those days long before a simple DNA test could prove or disprove such a claim. Kaighn expressed his opinion that Brown's constant stringing Bradley along had in fact made her mentally unbalanced: "I hated to [say] it, for Brown was one of my most intimate friends, but one cannot trifle with one's conscience." More than a hundred of Mr. Brown's letters to Mrs. Bradley were read in court, and if one cuts through his marked tendency to saccharine oratory, he certainly promised to marry her—repeatedly. To give just two examples of many, in one letter he wrote, "I will turn heaven and earth until I marry you," and another he signed "your husband." (He also had the temerity to complain that she was having a fling with an Englishman!)

When the day ended, Mrs. Bradley seemed a sympathetic figure to many. But not to all. The moralists at the *Louisville Courier-Journal* suggested that murderer and victim were equally to blame for the crime, and the only circumstance that made the case fascinating to the public was that the latter was a former senator: "The Bradley-Brown case tells the simple story of an affair in which there figured a woman whose age and experience in life had forced upon her a perfect knowledge of right and wrong, and a man who was untrue to his wife. . . . Possibly the woman was exceptionally weak and was 'lured.' More probably the two were fairly matched in guilt and accompanied one another from the straight path, neither leading and neither led."

On November 22, Mrs. Bradley's acquaintances and family members testified on her behalf to help answer the delicate question of why she had traveled all the way from Salt Lake City to Washington, DC, with a loaded and oiled horse pistol while on a mission to locate her reluctant lover. Her uncle related that "insanity and eccentricity" ran in the family; the former condition could have been relevant, the latter not since the term is so vague and subjective. (Senator Brown's law partner testified that Brown also was "eccentric.") The witnesses' testimony indicated that Mrs. Bradley was "distraught" and a "highly emotional" "nervous wreck" in the weeks (and even years) leading up to the murder. But being distraught, emotional, and nervous doesn't win acquittals.

Then the psychiatric experts weighed in on Mrs. Bradley's mental state. They were expected to answer a 13,000-word hypothetical question regarding Mrs. Bradley's sanity. (It would have been richly comical if one of the psychiatrists had replied, "Sorry, could you repeat the question?") This whopper of a query alone took two hours of court time to read aloud and included "eccentricity, insanity, or peculiar physical condition on the part of [Mrs. Bradley's] ancestors [to] try to force the conclusion that Mrs. Bradley was not responsible at the time of the tragedy." It sounds as if the defense, worried that they could not prove Mrs. Bradley's insanity, suggested her ancestors were crazy as the next best thing.

To achieve the agreeable purpose of turning Mrs. Bradley and her itchy trigger finger loose on the public, Dr. Wilfred Barton, Georgetown University's "expert on nervous diseases," testified on November 25 that she had suffered from "puerperal insanity" at the time she'd shot Brown. This implied that she had suffered from what we now call postpartum depression, but if so she'd had an unusually protracted case, since her second child by Brown was approaching four years in age. More likely, Dr. Barton was hinting that she had gone insane due to the alleged abortions Brown had performed on her. One interesting—and perhaps instructive—fact emerged: the allegedly frail, put-upon little Mrs. Bradley had once knocked Mr. Brown's front teeth out in a fight.

To laymen burdened with common sense, it seemed obvious that Mrs. Bradley had stalked Brown with the intention of killing him. The most generous interpretation was that she had meant to threaten him into marriage, had brought the gun as a means of gentle persuasion, and had shot him by accident. Dr. Barton for the defense, however, said that he found Mrs. Bradley to be "an abnormal woman." Asked what that meant specifically, he explained that "she was interested in things that do not usually attract women." As an example, Dr. Barton pointed out that she was absorbed in politics and was even secretary of a political club! This, plus the fact that she had some strange characters in her family tree, was the bulk of the evidence for her insanity plea.

A shrewd reporter observed that Mrs. Bradley "came into court . . . looking pale and haggard, evidently in anticipation that, after all, the question of her sanity or insanity at the time of the commission of the act was the paramount issue in the case." That is, Mrs. Bradley realized it was in her best interest to *look* crazy. On one occasion she acted as though in a stupor but forgot to stay in character and stole anxious glances at the jurors' faces.

On November 27, the prosecution had its turn to present witnesses who argued that Mrs. Bradley was as sane as you please and always had been. Practically everyone who'd had any contact with her immediately after the shooting, including hotel staff, police officers, doctors, and reporters, testified that she had been rational and coherent. Ditto from people who'd spoken with her in Salt Lake City before her ill-fated train trip to Washington. Interestingly, neither the prosecution nor the defense called as a witness Anna C. Adams, whose letters to Brown appear to have been the catalyst for Mrs. Bradley ventilating his abdomen. Why neither side thought it was worth getting Adams's almost certainly relevant testimony on the record is one of the case's unsolved mysteries.

Closing arguments began on November 30. The assistant DA told the jury to "cast aside all sentiment and treat the case exactly as if a man had done the shooting." (In retrospect, he might as well have told them to wish themselves to Saturn.) He pointed out the paucity of evidence that Mrs. Bradley had been insane when she'd shot Brown. Everyone admitted that Brown was a less than stellar human being, said the prosecution, but that didn't give Mrs. Bradley the right to avenge herself via murder.

The defense countered that the abortions Brown had forced upon Bradley had resulted in a septic infection that led to insanity, the symptoms of which, mysteriously, she had not displayed before the shooting. Attorney Robert Wells argued that his client must have been temporarily insane because she'd killed the man she loved. One wonders how well that argument would have fared if used to defend a man who had killed a woman he loved. Mrs. Bradley responded to this eloquence by toppling forward as though in a faint.

The prosecution responded that Bradley was more annoyed than insane: "Of course she was disturbed, but who wouldn't be? If you can't find any evidence of insanity up to the time of the shooting and none since then, it is a strong presumption that she was sane at the time charged in the indictment." The prosecution refused to wallow in sentimental drivel about broken promises and shattered hearts, calling both Brown and Bradley homewreckers.

The jury entered deliberations on December 2. Their verdict, which came the next day to a round of courtroom applause, was no surprise to anyone: acquittal! No doubt the jurors fancied themselves knights in shining armor helping a persecuted damsel in distress who once had knocked the teeth out of her noncommittal lover. The *Courier-Journal* commented, "She was presented to the members [of the jury] as a suffering, misused, tormented, ruined soul; a wreck of a woman whose life had been shattered by the man whom she loved. . . . The role was played to a finish. The fact that she was no infant in arms, innocent, trusting and blushing, cut no figure. Her sophistication and deliberateness, her minimum of scruples, her willful and open living in adultery with her victim counted for little."

But Mrs. Bradley's melodrama was not entirely finished. She returned to Salt Lake City, where she found that her former friends were less forgiving of her little indiscretion than that Washington jury had been. Only a month after her acquittal she was penniless and living in a shack on the city's outskirts with her four children—two by her former lawful husband, two the illegitimate children of Senator Brown. "She returned believing that she would be received with open arms," said a newspaper report. However, she cried, "I am more in prison now than I was in Washington." These friends who no longer desired her company were all female, which suggests that women of the era were less easily suckered than men by the sentiment surrounding murder.

Although she had been undeniably, comprehensively, and insultingly cut out of the senator's will, in February 1910 Mrs. Bradley decided to take a shot at getting some of that Brown money after all. She filed suit to have her two children declared legally Brown's and therefore entitled to a share of his vast $70,000 estate. In September the court declared that Bradley's two sons would receive $6,000 apiece; the modern equivalent would be slightly over $115,000 for each.

Mrs. Bradley's supernatural patience had paid off at last!

Remorseful Killers

John S. appears to have been made of finer stuff than the average highway robber. On January 6, 1904, two men were shot to death on a road near Salt Lake City. The mystery lasted only until January 10, when John made a full confession.

He said that he had not meant to kill his victims—robbery had been his only intention. But they had put up such a fight that he'd shot them in self-defense. Overcome with guilt, John had contemplated suicide but didn't have the nerve to go through with it.

John told the police that he was the heir to "considerable property" and to make partial amends, he wanted to sign it over to the families of his victims.

In a similar incident, Spencer M. disappeared in Enterprise, a town fifty miles northwest of St. George, on March 18, 1935. A year later Spencer's wife got a divorce on grounds of desertion and married twenty-four-year-old shepherd Charley B.

In November 1937, Charley confessed that he had killed Spencer with a pipe over the head when the latter had attacked him in a drunken fury. Charley hid the body in an abandoned well 110 feet deep. (He was aided in corpse disposal by the dead man's brother-in-law. Spencer seems not to have been too well-liked.) Charley married his victim's widow because he "felt a sense of responsibility toward her" and her son. He added that neither his wife nor his adopted son knew that he had murdered Spencer.

Sheriff Antone Prince checked out the well on November 19 and found the body of Spencer inside, as promised. The sheriff had quite the adventure when Spencer's head was accidentally pulled off by the team dragging the body out with a rope. Prince had to go down the well to retrieve it.

Charley claimed self-defense and certainly did the right thing by his victim's widow, but murder charges were filed against him and Spencer's brother-in-law.

"I'll stand by you, Charley, right to the end," said his wife. As it turned out, the jury accepted Charley's defense, and in January 1938 he was acquitted.

An Uncommonly Stupid Murder

After the Union Pacific train rolled into Ogden on March 15, 1924, a sharp-eyed baggage man noticed dried blood on the hinges of a trunk that was bound for Weed, California. Railroad officials steeled themselves and opened the lid. They found exactly what they were afraid they'd see, an object that never fails to get undivided attention and make an impression: a headless woman clad only in silk underwear, a silk kimono, and bedroom slippers. A piece of rag carpet was in the trunk too, and when the officials peeked under it a woman's head stared sightlessly back at them.

The murder wasn't exactly a professional job. The killer had been so flighty as to include the head in the trunk instead of sensibly disposing of it, and its distinguishing marks made first-rate clues: the victim was thirty to thirty-five years old and had false upper teeth, blue eyes, and dark brown hair. The rest of the body revealed she was extremely small, measuring about four feet, ten inches in height and weighing a hundred pounds.

Shipping records showed that the trunk had been mailed from Denver. Dr. Roy Wilson, Ogden's city physician, determined that the woman had been killed within the last couple of days. When detectives opened the disembodied head's mouth, they found a man's handkerchief bearing the monogrammed letter F.

Therefore! The first items of business were to send a telegram to Denver police and inquire whether any man with the initial F had shipped a trunk from that city sometime on or around March 14 and whether a petite woman with false upper teeth was missing from the vicinity. Sometimes detective work is really easy.

These instructive facts were learned in short order: former church janitor Fred Janssen and his wife, Bella, had been missing from their Denver apartment since the night of March 13; the description of the body was a perfect match for Mrs. Janssen; and an inspection of their apartment yielded a bloody carpet. Also, Mr. Janssen had taken out a $1,000 insurance policy on Mrs. Janssen only a month before, but no doubt that was just a coincidence.

Fred Janssen was nabbed in Eden, Colorado, on March 17. Perhaps he realized denial was futile; perhaps he was embarrassed at having been caught so easily after committing an uncommonly stupid murder. In any case, once captured he sang like a wood thrush. He admitted that his wife had been murdered while she was praying and that he had hired a Mexican to do the dirty work; also, he said he had absented himself from the room during the action, presumably because he didn't want to see it.

Fred went on trial on April 8. Three days later he was given a life sentence at the Colorado State Penitentiary in Canon City. Who exactly out in Weed, California, was supposed to pick up the trunk after it was delivered and what he was expected to do with its contents were never made clear.

Lost Treasure, Lost Life

In 1893 two prospectors exploring the bottom of a shaft near Park City found a pair of heavy work boots. Sheathed within them were skeletal feet. Rats had long since consumed the flesh of the dead miner, and the elements had done the same to his clothing. A note was found near the corpse, reading, "Dear God, I am dying. I have found wealth at the cost of my life. The samples in the bucket are from a ledge on—my hand trembles, my eyes grow dim—I—I am . . ."

The bucket referred to in the note was an old lunch pail bearing the initials R. S. When the miners looked in it, they found chunks of gold ore.

7

ABNORMAL ARIZONA

Super Skeletons

In November 1921, miner August E. found the bones of a race of giants after heavy rains at Redington unearthed them. The skeletons seemed double the size of the average modern man, and one perfectly preserved skull was made of bone an inch thick. The rain also revealed pottery, earrings, and remains of charcoal.

Pickup Service Requested

An officer in Bisbee received a curious telephone call at the police station on February 25, 1913. "This is Jim C.," said the caller. "Come here and get me. I'm dead."

The officer rushed to the caller's residence and found the fresh remains of Jim, who had just shot himself. The bloody receiver still dangled from the phone.

Not a Deadbeat

The Bronco mine, three miles southeast of Tombstone, was reportedly haunted in summer 1897 by "a tall white form" that appeared every night two hours after sunset. It walked in the adobe shanty near the mouth of the main shaft but vanished when approached too closely. According to one account, "Many of the mountaineers and plainsmen of the neighborhood have shot at him time and again, and often from very close range," to no effect.

But the ghost wasn't all bad; it had a work ethic that would put most living men to shame. Instead of resting after scaring people for a few hours nightly, at midnight it went into the mine and *worked*: "For hours he has been heard working in the deserted drifts, now pounding drills, now sawing timbers and sometimes blasting."

No fewer than sixteen men were murdered in the Bronco mine, so identifying the ghost might be as difficult a task as figuring out how it got access to dynamite.

Vintage Violence: Executions and Lynchings

Tucson was appalled by the murders of pawnbroker Vicente Hernandez and his wife, which occurred on the night of August 20, 1873. Their skulls were pulverized with a club and their jugular veins slit. The next day, citizens offered a $900 reward.

Leonardo Cordova was arrested in short order. He not only confessed, but he named two accomplices: Clemente Lopez and Jesus Saquaripa, who admitted their guilt. They also revealed where they had hidden the loot stolen from Hernandez, which clinched matters.

Lynching fever was in the air. Someone suggested that in addition to the three killers, they might as well also hang John Willis, who had been arrested for murdering Robert Swope at Sanford in November 1872 and who already had been sentenced to a legal execution. The citizens responded, "Well, why not?"

Two tall forked posts were driven into the ground near the jail, forked ends pointing upward. A twelve-foot-long pole was slid through the tops of the posts, and ropes were tied to the structure to give it strength and support. The four blindfolded prisoners were led out and placed on the bed of a wagon under the horizontal pole; nooses were tied; a horse drew the wagon out from under them, and four men swung side by side in the Tucson sun.

The coroner's official verdict: it was society's fault. He said, "[The men] were hung by the people of Tucson en masse, in view of the terrible crimes and murders committed, and the tardiness of justice—the inevitable result of allowing criminals to escape the penalties of their crimes."

One of Cochise County's most notorious incidents is the Bisbee Massacre, in which several outlaws killed four citizens while robbing a general store on December 8, 1883. Five were tried and executed at Tombstone on March 28, 1884. The point is inevitably made that the five were the first men to be *legally* hanged in Tombstone. There was no such good fortune for the massacre's mastermind, John Heath, who was sentenced to life in prison at the Yuma Penitentiary on February 21, 1884.

Within twenty-four hours of the sentence being passed, an estimated 150 vigilantes, mostly miners, seized Heath from his jail cell and carried him to a telegraph pole at the foot of Tombstone's Toughnut Street. Heath told his audience that he didn't mind being hanged too much but requested that they not shoot at his body after the deed was done. They agreed to honor his final request, and within moments Heath was dancing in the air. Someone with an admirable appreciation for historical dates stuck a note on the telegraph pole: "John Heath was hanged to this pole by citizens of Cochise County for participation in the Bisbee massacre, as a proved accessory, at 8:20 a.m., Feb. 22, 1884 (Washington's Birthday), to advance Arizona."

The coroner's jury's verdict was a small masterpiece of dark humor: they ruled that Heath had died of emphysema, "which might have been caused by strangulation, self-inflicted or otherwise."

Edwin W. Hawkins murdered Albert Leonhardt in November 1907. He spent time in his Tucson cell recording phonographic messages to his mother, wife, and sister so they'd have something to remember him by after his hanging. His sister sent Hawkins a letter stating, "If I were there that would not happen"—by which she meant that if she could, she would gladly kill Edwin and save him the indignity of going to the gallows. It was a matter of family honor, perhaps.

Hawkins swung for his crime on August 14, 1908. Unlike most hangings, it was neither quick nor clean: Hawkins's neck did not break, and he swung, strangling, for fourteen minutes.

A Phoenix mob numbering a hundred was so determined to lynch murderer Starr Daley that they pursued lawmen who were trying to spirit Daley away for forty miles over rough desert terrain in the middle of the night—not on horses but in automobiles, since the date was May 5, 1917. The mob caught up with the officers just a mile from their destination, the safety of the prison at Florence. They unceremoniously snatched Daley and returned him to the scene of his crime.

When Daley saw the end was near, he confessed to the murder for which he had been convicted—that of James Ray Gibson—and two others of which he had not been suspected. He showed the mob how to properly adjust the rope so that his neck would be instantly broken.

The mob offered a prayer as Daley knelt in the back seat of a car and moaned, "Oh my God." Then he was hanged from an electric power pole rather than the to-be-expected tree limb. He was buried at the site, not unlike a dead mongrel.

Governor Thomas Campbell had been called at 1:00 a.m. and informed that the lynching was about to take place. He rushed from his house with two aides in hopes of reasoning with the mob, but when he arrived he was greeted by the unlovely sight of Daley swinging from that power pole.

The coroner's jury's verdict: justifiable homicide!

The warden of the Arizona State Penitentiary at Florence got in trouble in December 1924 for exhuming the bodies of two hanged men, Paul V. Hadley and Theodore West, removing their heads, and sending the disembodied domes to "experts in criminology at the Carnegie Institute" who wanted to study them.

Jack Sullivan went to the gas chamber in Florence on May 15, 1936. When asked if he had a final request, he said, "Sure, you might bring me a gas mask."

Earl Gardner, an Apache, stabbed a fellow tribesman to death in 1925, for which he spent seven years in prison. He earned the tribal name Ne-pau-kee-seyi, or "The Killer." Having learned nothing from his imprisonment, he killed his wife and baby with an ax on December 8, 1935. Gardner craved to be hanged—indeed, he insisted upon it—and was infuriated when the Circuit Court of Appeals delayed his execution. On June 17, 1936, when a judge sentenced him to hang for the second time, the prisoner accused him of lying: "I don't believe you. You didn't kill me the last time you said you were going to."

Gardner's fondest wish came true on July 13 in San Carlos. But the execution was a botched job: Gardner's fall was broken when his body hit the side of the trap as he dropped; also, the noose's knot slid to the front of his throat. He dangled more than a half hour before his life was extinct. Before the hanging Gardner had boasted that he would take his punishment "like an Apache."

Frank Rascon, a Mexican cowboy, went to the gas chamber in Phoenix on July 10, 1936. When the room was cleared of gas, Rascon's distraught wife embraced his body and showered him with kisses—after which she became seriously ill. The gas left trace amounts of cyanide on the dead man's lips.

Gallows Humor

Arizona's Old Yuma Territorial Prison was opened in 1876 and still exists as a tourist attraction. Better still, the place is supposedly haunted.

Like most prisons of the era, it had a cemetery for convenient disposal of naturally deceased prisoners and the executed. One of the latter was scheduled to be hanged on a gallows erected in the graveyard. Spectators noticed that he grinned broadly as the rope was adjusted around his neck. When asked what was so darn funny, he replied, "Well, I was just thinking. You guys have got to walk back up there in this heat. I don't."

Dead Man's Drink

Outlaw John Shaw and an accomplice entered the Wigwam Saloon in Winslow on April 8, 1905, ostensibly to get a drink of whiskey. Instead, they grabbed over $250 worth of silver dollars from a gambling table and lammed it out of there. Lawmen had no difficulty tracking the clumsy thieves: they left a trail of coins as they fled to the train tracks. The Navajo County sheriff and his deputy found Shaw and his friend in Canyon Diablo, twenty-five miles from town.

An epic shootout commenced between the four men, sometimes at such close range that they were only four feet apart. The sheriff finally sent a bullet through Shaw's head. He was buried with haste in the Canyon Diablo cemetery. His injured accomplice wound up in Yuma Prison.

But Shaw's story doesn't end there. The next night, a group of drunken cowpokes at the Wigwam Saloon decided they wanted to make Shaw's acquaintance. It didn't bother them so much that Shaw and his companion had stolen from the saloon; no, what troubled them was that after stealing the money, Shaw had run off into the night without finishing the whiskey he had ordered. They were determined that Shaw should have that final drink.

Brandishing whiskey bottles, they boarded the train, staggered to the cemetery, exhumed the outlaw's pine coffin, and removed its occupant. They poured the "devil's anesthetic" down his gullet. One of the cowboys had borrowed a camera and took a series of photos showing his intoxicated friends holding up Shaw, who—judging from his awkward pose and the stiffness of his arms—must have been undergoing rigor mortis. The photos also prove that he had died wearing a big sappy grin. Something funny must have occurred to him in his final seconds. The gentle and refined but curious reader may see the pictures in the book *True Tales and Amazing Legends of the Old West* by the editors of *True West Magazine*.

After treating Shaw, the cowboys said a prayer and placed him back in his coffin—with a whiskey bottle—and covered his grave, so as not to be thought disrespectful.

Getting Rattled

Arizona has never been noted for lacking rattlesnakes, but certain areas were blessed with a bumper crop of the reptiles in September 1898. A visitor from the region, G. R. Kenton, regaled the *Washington Post*: "Not long since, they invaded a mining camp in the section near where I live, and during their brief sojourn a regular reign of terror existed." Snakes got into miners' cabins and found human beds to be inviting places to rest. People fortunate enough to have two-story houses stayed upstairs when the sun went down. In Kingman, people crowded into a bandstand and pavilion and slumbered there rather than risk sleeping on the ground.

To perpetrate a brilliant pun, the snake invasion had Arizonans feeling rattled. It was theorized that the summer of 1898 was so hot, even by Arizona standards, that the snakes sought the shade of the great indoors.

Lawson's Leaving

Editors have always loved sensational stories that sell newspapers, and the papers of old often were far more graphic than one might expect. Gruesome suicides were the special joy of reporters. A typical stomach-turning example is the *Arizona Republican*'s gory account of the tragic end of Lawson F., who shot himself in the head while contemplating his reflection in a mirror on September 8, 1893.

The paper referred to Lawson's death chamber as "the bloodiest and ghastliest place of death ever witnessed in Phoenix" and to Lawson himself as "the ghastliest corpse ever seen in the city"—and that was just in the headline and the first paragraph. But these phrases were rainbows and lollipops compared to the no-holds-barred description of the mess

Lawson left behind, a catalogue of horrors that reads more like autopsy notes than a news report:

> A hole in the head, through which daylight could be seen; a plaster of blood and brains and hair spread upon the ceiling by the fatal charge; the bloodstained and brain bespattered gun barrels; the prostrate form; the open mouth, in and out of which flies were crawling; the gaping wound, within which other flies were making explorations; the torn and shredded scalp; a bloody sore under the chin which had eaten away the flesh, disclosing the veins of the throat, a mark of the disease which induced the suicide; the squalid surroundings of this scene of self-butchery, presented a picture of which those who saw it carried away a sickening recollection.

Reading the description of the scene was the next best thing to actually seeing it. The writer then noted that a doctor "made a professional examination of the corpse," though it certainly sounds as though the journalist already had done that himself. A coroner's jury was assembled but had to be reconvened since one member left for a dance during a brief adjournment; scrutinizing Lawson's body must have made him really feel like cutting a rug. At last the jury determined that Lawson was dead. Not that their services were strictly necessary.

A Subterranean Swede

McCabe in Yavapai County has been a ghost town since 1917. One of its more mysterious denizens was a Swedish miner and hermit named Oscar Johnson. As if he didn't get his fill of digging for gold on his claim, he also dug a well on his property at the end of a long backbreaking day. Neighbors were baffled because he kept *on* digging that well long after logic dictated that he should have been finished with it. Not only that, but Johnson made more trips to his well at night than would be expected from a man of average thirst. Naturally, other McCabe residents thought he might have a secret gold mine or at least was hiding his loot down in the well, but the reclusive Swede refused to satisfy their curiosity on this or any other point.

Johnson seldom made trips to town, but the day came when people realized they had not seen him in a while, nor had smoke curled from his cabin's chimney.

Some miners took a ladder and descended into the well. They found Johnson's secret, or at least part of it: he had dug a side tunnel opening into a large room in which he had spent considerable time. But there was no trace of Oscar. Neither he, his possessions, nor his money were found that day or ever. His fate remains a mystery.

Not to get anyone's hopes up, but legend holds that Johnson's treasure is still buried in McCabe.

Ed's Humor

Prospector Ed Schieffelin, one of Arizona's noted pioneers, was determined to found a town in the desert. His friends hooted, "All you're gonna find out there is your tombstone."

Schieffelin did establish a town, and because he had an advanced sense of irony he named it Tombstone. The town went on to become the stuff of American legend. Schieffelin died on May 12, 1897, and as a further display of dry humor his first grave marker read "This is my Tombstone."

8

UNNATURAL NEW MEXICO

Self-Made Monument

Among the nearly forty thousand identical government-issue tombstones in Santa Fe National Cemetery, there is one grave marker that stands out. It is a sandstone statue of a soldier resting under a tree stump, complete with hat and uniform. The inscription reads, "Dennis O'Leary, Pvt., Co. 1, 23 Infty, died Apl. 1, 1901. Age 23 yrs & 9 mos."

The unconfirmed legend goes that Private O'Leary went AWOL for several weeks while serving at Fort Wingate. When he returned, he refused to say where he had been and served time in the stockade.

On April 1, 1901, Private O'Leary committed suicide. He left a note giving directions to his monument, which he had sculpted singlehandedly in the mountains, along with a request that the statue be placed on his grave.

When his fellow soldiers found the statue, they saw that the death date of April 1, 1901, had already been chiseled on it by O'Leary. Suicide on a certain date had been his plan all along. He'd probably spent his time while AWOL creating the monument.

Billy the Kidnapped?

The life and legend of the notorious gunslinger Billy the Kid (aka Henry McCarty, William Bonney) are so famous that only a cursory summary is necessary: born in Manhattan; migrated to New Mexico; joined the side of rancher John Tunstall in the famous Lincoln County War; killed between eight and eleven men (depending on who's counting); a nice enough young fellow, except when he was killing you; shot at age twenty-one by Sheriff Pat Garrett on July 14, 1881. But there is another fact about Billy that appears to be practically unknown: according to a contemporary source, his body was snatched from the grave a few days after burial. The cemetery's by far most famous resident may not actually be there.

In September or October 1881, a newspaper called the *Las Vegas* [NM] *Optic* made the claim, which was reprinted in the *Louisville Courier-Journal* on October 19. According to their story, Billy was buried on July 16 in the Fort Sumner cemetery in De Baca County. Billy's rest was brief: on the night of July 21 a ghoul from San Miguel County skulked into the graveyard, exhumed him, and carried him away in a wagon. He took the gunfighter's remains to the office of an unnamed local doctor, who removed the head and boiled it, thereby removing the skin and rendering the skull of the already notorious Billy the Kid a highly collectible souvenir. Supposedly the rest of the body was buried in a corral, where the doctor intended to leave it until it had naturally decomposed. His plan was to exhume the bones, wire them together, varnish them, and have a complete Kid.

One wonders how the reporter at the *Optic* tumbled onto this dastardly plot but also why he would make such a sensational and easily disproved claim if it wasn't true. All that was necessary to prove the truth or falsity of the story was to grab a shovel and dig. If a hoax, it would be grounds for a libel suit, as it should not have been difficult to guess the identity of the doctor involved. How many physicians could there have been in Las Vegas, NM, in 1881?

Assuming the story were true, what did the doctor plan to do with the skeleton? The best guess is that he, or some entrepreneur, wanted to take it on tour so gawkers could enjoy its company for a nickel a head, the occasional fate of dead outlaws (i.e., Elmer McCurdy and Rube Burrow). If this was the case, evidently the body was not put on public display. Why is anyone's guess.

One might think it would settle the question if forensic investigators were to open the grave. However, while there is still a marker for the Kid at Fort Sumner, the exact location of his grave is not certain. The Pecos River flooded in September 1904, washing away the original wooden headstone. His grave remained unmarked until 1932. The riddle of the grave's precise whereabouts—and its contents, if any—may never be solved.

Tomb Raiders

In October 1924, the National Geographic Society explored the tombs of prehistoric Native Americans at Pueblo Bonito in Chaco Canyon. In three burial chambers, they found sixty-five unburied skeletons, all in a "disturbed condition." Some were dismembered, others headless. Heads were found tossed in a corner or lined up along a wall.

Who had performed these disgraceful, disrespectful acts? A major clue was that, unlike in pristine crypts, there were no turquoise ornaments.

The victims were ancient Indians and so were the ghouls, probably rival tribes on the prowl for jewelry. Luckily, they didn't raid the deeper graves, and the society discovered treasures of art, jewels, and domestic tools.

Taking a Wrong Turn at Albuquerque

Random tragedy seemed to strike Albuquerque pharmacist Carl W. on November 25, 1933: while he and his fourth wife, Donalda, were on their honeymoon, she was found dead in the road with a dented head. Carl said she had been killed by a hit-and-run driver, and by the way, when do I get paid her $1,000 life insurance? Carl's overall demeanor troubled investigators, and they held him for questioning until they got autopsy results.

It was a good thing they held him, too, because police in two other states were very interested in Carl—a chubby, bespectacled thirty-four-year-old who looked considerably older—after reading about him in the newspapers. He had married his third wife, Marie B. in Vici, Oklahoma, in November 1931. The couple went to Holbrook, Arizona, and Marie died two months later. Marie was the subject of an autopsy that, unfortunately, was conducted *after* she was embalmed. Her internal organs were crammed with poison, but authorities thought it might have gotten there via the magic of embalming, so Carl wasn't charged. In the wake of Donalda's death, an Oklahoma investigator looked closely into the matter of Marie's demise, and the undertaker told him "no mineral poison was contained in the embalming fluid used." Also, Carl had collected $2,000 worth of life insurance on Marie.

Meanwhile, Colorado detectives were curious about Carl's second wife, Rhoda K., whom he had married in Brighton in 1930 and insured for $2,000. Police thought her death, which occurred after she drank a concoction mixed by her druggist husband, was suspicious and did an investigation, but no charges were filed.

Carl's *first* wife, Mina M. of Edmond, Oklahoma, had married him in 1926. He had abandoned her just hours after their son was born. She divorced Carl a few months later, and in retrospect this seems a wise decision.

Three wives dead in three years? What were the odds?

On December 1, Carl confessed that he had killed Donalda with a tire iron. The motive was an insurance payout, as many had suspected all along. The reader will observe Carl's increasing greed and impatience: he waited a while before killing wife number two and got away with it despite skeptical murmurs; he killed his third wife after only two months of matrimony and drew even more suspicion on himself; when he killed his fourth wife, he was so overconfident that he murdered her right away. He *thought* no one would notice.

The three-time murderer's first wife, the one that got away, remarked, "I have been waiting a long time for this, because I knew something would catch up with Carl sooner or later."

That "something" was New Mexico's electric chair. Carl was scheduled to park his pants there on June 8, 1934, but he received a stay of execution, and his sentence was commuted.

Murder by Horse

It was a needlessly complicated way to commit murder, but that didn't make it any less effective. On the night of October 24, 1911, someone abducted Mrs. Juan D. from her ranch near San Rafael, bound her as she lay on the ground to a bronco tied to a stake—a news report made certain to note that the horse was "ugly"—and whipped the bronco until it was maddened to a frenzy, then released it.

Mrs. D.'s body was found two days later. Western movies usually make getting dragged by a horse seem like a minor inconvenience. This is the reality: "Her shapeless corpse, barely recognizable, was found with the broken lariat knotted on her neck." They found the horse later, still smarting from its whipping.

Who could have done such a fiendish deed? Well, the lariat and saddle on the horse belonged to the dead woman's husband, a wealthy rancher. He recently had been infuriated when he'd beheld her dancing with another man at a ball. After the murder he was nowhere in the vicinity, and he was spotted boarding a train at Los Lunas, a hundred miles from San Rafael. So the smart money was on Mr. D.

Those Practical Westerners

The citizens of Las Vegas dug a well in 1876 and, with considerable optimism, constructed a large windmill over it. The idea was to pump out water, but within months the well went dry. Las Vegas was left with a big, seemingly useless structure.

At least it was seemingly useless until June 5, 1879, when vigilantes looking for a convenient place from which to hang Manuel Barela and Giovanni Dugi realized the windmill made a jim-dandy location for a lynching. The next morning townspeople awoke to find more than birds roosting on the mill.

Lynchers hanged three more from the structure on February 8, 1880. Law-abiding citizens were not pleased and tore the windmill down in April. According to *True West* writer Mark Boardman, a gazebo is now on the site where the windmill once stood. Five men were hanged there—something to think about as you contemplate the view and eat corn dogs.

Taking a Dip

Rancher and sheepman Solomon Luna was the wealthiest man in the state and has been called "the father of New Mexico's statehood." New Mexicans wanted him to be their first senator, but he declined.

He died under mysterious circumstances on a Horse Springs ranch on August 29, 1912. He was found scalded in a vat containing thousands of gallons of lime, water, tobacco, and sulfur, a noxious mixture used to disinfect sheep. The boiling fluid had peeled the flesh from his face and hands, and he wore only his hat, shoes, and underwear.

The coroner's jury deemed it an accidental death, a verdict that provokes controversy to this day. Some observers thought Luna had committed suicide in a particularly grotesque fashion. Hispanic friends thought he had been murdered. However, he had no known enemies and had complained of a weak heart for several days prior.

The course of history may be affected by such a strange, seemingly random event. Luna was New Mexico's most prominent Republican; after his death, the party lost strength in the state. As a result, Democrat Woodrow Wilson carried New Mexico in the 1912 presidential election and gained three electoral votes. This is not to say William Howard Taft would have won the presidency if Luna had not died, but if Theodore Roosevelt had not additionally drawn votes away from Taft, who knows?

Mr. Kennedy Proves a Bad Host

Elizabethtown is now a ghost town, and Charles Kennedy had a prominent hand in contributing to the stock of ghosts. Kennedy, a boardinghouse operator who seemed always to have a vacant room for Elizabethtown's miners and visitors, lived in the nearby village of Eagle Nest. Wayfaring strangers would come to town, rent a room, and then never be seen again. This was not considered suspicious, as it was assumed the boarders were passing through on the way to Taos.

But one day in autumn 1870, a missing renter's friends became suspicious and headed for the Kennedy residence, the last place he was known to be. On the way they met a highly contrite Mrs. Kennedy, a Ute Indian, who confessed all she knew. And she knew plenty!

A number of men hastily gathered, and when they entered Mr. Kennedy's fine establishment without knocking first they found the proprietor burning bits and pieces of the missing traveler in a fire. The dead man's valuables were gathered in a pile on the floor. Investigators later found other burned or buried corpses on the property.

Kennedy survived until his pretrial date on October 3, 1870, but on October 7 a lynch mob—headed by none other than noted gunfighter Clay Allison, then a New Mexican rancher—carried Kennedy out of the courthouse, tied a rope around his neck, and dragged him from a horse that galloped up and down Main Street. After the undertaker scooped up what remained of the remains, angry townspeople refused to allow Kennedy a proper burial in the cemetery. The most hated man in town was buried on the graveyard's outer boundary. No one knows how many travelers he had robbed and murdered, but estimates range as low as fourteen and as high as one hundred.

What happened to his victims' money, gold, and valuables? It's a mystery, though the loot is rumored to be buried in a cache in the Sangre de Cristo Mountains.

Lynchings

According to historian Marc Simmons, lynching bees were so common in pioneer Socorro that the vigilantes were known collectively as Los Colgadores ("the hangers"). Simmons relates the example of violent, alcoholic rancher John (or Joe) Fowler, who was suspected of murdering his workers so he could cheat them out of their pay. His most public killing was the one that got him in trouble: in 1883, he slashed the belly of an unoffending man in the Grand Central Hotel. Fowler's attorney, Neil B. Field, heard ugly rumors of an impending lynching and promised the court, "If one hair on Mr. Fowler's head is touched, I will leave Socorro forever!" Evidently the toughs were untroubled by the town being short one lawyer, and that night they seized Fowler from his cell, tied a rope around his neck, and yanked him upward.

One of Socorro's more obnoxious late-nineteenth-century citizens was an immigrant called Russian Bill, who had a fatal weakness for practical jokes. Residents stood it as long as they could, until Bill simply went too far in the hotel one Christmas Eve. Under the influence, he ventured into the card room and proved his marksmanship by shooting the finger off a gambler. The disgusted card players seized Bill and hanged him from the hotel dining room's ceiling rafters on the charge of "being a damn nuisance."

But was there more than one Russian Bill? It is a matter of historical record that on November 7, 1881, a horse thief called "Russian Bill" Tettenborn (or Tattenbaum) was hanged, alongside one Sandy King, from the rafters of the Grant House Dining Room in Shakespeare, due to the lack of a convenient tree. Mr. King was lynched for shooting the finger off a haberdashery clerk. Allegedly, a witty coroner's jury ruled that the men died "from a shortage of breath due to a sudden change in altitude." Rather than cut down the bodies, the Vigilance Committee left them swinging so passengers who disembarked from the next stagecoach would have something to write home about. One of the passengers toted Russian Bill to the cemetery in exchange for the dead man's boots.

After Bill was buried, the postmaster of Shakespeare received a letter from a woman in Russia asking how her son was faring. No doubt wishing to break the news gently, yet unable to resist indulging in the dark humor endemic to the frontier, this circumspect government official wrote back, "Dear Madam, I am sorry to report that your son has died of throat trouble."

The reader will note a similarity in certain details in the Socorro and Shakespeare incidents. Either the stories got confused somewhere along the line or New Mexico was once full of Russian Bills whom the citizenry, singularly lacking in fingers, lynched from hotel ceilings.

9

INCREDIBLE IDAHO

Laughing Last

John N., aka "Bohemian John," was a hunter and trapper in the mountains of Idaho. One day the partial remains of two men were found in the woods—they were unidentifiable, having been gnawed on by a grizzly bear, but one of them was thought to be John and given a proper burial.

When John turned up alive three years later, no one believed he was the real article. "Bohemian John is dead," they said. "He's buried out in the cemetery." John ventured to the graveyard and saw the monument reading "Sacred to the memory of Bohemian John. Killed by a bear."

John had the last laugh three times over. Not only was he alive when everyone believed him dead, he removed his gravestone from the cemetery and raffled it. In addition, he had to pay no taxes in Idaho since he was legally dead there. As of December 1904, he was working in the Midas mine near Redding, California.

Ungrateful James

Young James W. lived on a ranch near Sarilda, Fremont County. One fine day in August 1912, his mother asked him to help turn the wringer as she did the family laundry. James didn't wanna, and he got spanked for his refusal. He argued with Mrs. W. by swiping Pa's shotgun and instantly killing her. He showed not a scintilla of remorse afterward.

James was only eleven years old, but that didn't save him from being arrested, tried, found guilty, and sentenced to ten to fifty years in prison.

One account noted that he wore a striped outfit like the other convicts, but his was made with knee breeches à la Buster Brown, the fashion for smartly dressed lads of the era.

The boy now known as Prisoner Number 1949 had the dubious honor of being placed in a cell near Albert Horsley (alias Harry Orchard), who had assassinated former governor Frank Steunenberg in 1905. However, he was not allowed to circulate with the older convicts. The record does not state whether the warden thought they would be a bad influence on James or vice versa.

James spent most of his time in the institution's library, where his education was furthered by the librarian, the only inmate he was allowed to have contact with. So James took lessons in prison just as if he were in school. (Insert your own mordant joke here!) His other special privileges were that he could play with the warden's children and the jail's bloodhounds. At 5:00 p.m. every day, however, he was expected to be back in his cell.

I was unable to find out whether James served a full fifty-year sentence, let alone the minimum ten years, but somehow it seems doubtful.

The Blackest of Black Widows, or: Arsenic and Young Lace

Hawaii is a beautiful place to visit, but it isn't so much fun getting arrested there. No doubt Paul Vincent Southard, chief petty officer on the USS *Chicago*, wondered what the Honolulu authorities wanted with his wife, Lyda, when they arrested her on May 12, 1921. Poor Paul was due for some surprises.

For one thing, he wasn't Lyda's first husband; he was her fifth, and she had found time for all this matrimonial action despite being merely twenty-eight years old. Also, she had committed murder six times, and the majority of her victims were former husbands. According to Idaho deputy sheriff Virgil S. Ormsby, who had spent two years tracking her down, this was her story.

She had been born Lyda (or Lydia) Anna Mae Trueblood in Keytesville, Missouri, on October 16, 1892. When barely out of her teens, she had moved to Twin Falls, Idaho, soon followed by two Keytesville neighbors, brothers Robert and Edward Dooley. Robert married her in 1912. The bride talked her husband and brother-in-law into insuring themselves for $2,000 total, with her as a beneficiary. In the event that either Dooley died, half the money would go to Lyda. Edward took ill of "typhoid fever" (note sarcastic quotation marks) on August 9, 1915, and he boarded the

Stygian ferry several days later. His body was shipped back to Keytesville. It was all very sad, but Lyda was enriched to the tune of a thousand big boys. Her husband got the other $1,000.

Having a windfall was *so* nice, said Lyda to poor unsuspecting Robert; why don't we insure *ourselves* for $2,000, the money to go to the survivor? He took her advice. Like night follows day, he came down with "typhoid" after drinking from a well on their property and found a permanent job at the dust factory on October 1. He was sent to Keytesville to keep his brother company under the sod, and Lyda was $3,000 to the better, possibly $4,000 if she got to keep the thousand bucks Robert had received when Edward died. It seems likely, since he hadn't had much time to spend it.

Lyda and Robert were the parents of an infant daughter named Loraine, whom Lyda said also had imbibed water from the infected well, and the concerned mother expressed fear that the child might die of "typhoid." That she did on November 15, making Lyda $500 wealthier and free to start life anew. No one seems to have asked how she avoided catching the dread disease since she presumably drank from the same well as the rest of the family.

In 1917, Lyda married William McHaffie, a Twin Falls waiter. She insured his life for $5,000 on June 12, after which the happy couple moved to Hardin, Montana. About a year later, he was laid low by "influenza," according to his death certificate. Lyda didn't get rich this time, but not through lack of trying. She had forgotten to pay the premiums, and the insurance company refused to give her the five grand, even though she belatedly offered to pay her debt. She did not seem to understand that this would be akin to buying fire insurance after the house had caught fire.

The grieving widow—who was probably really grieving over that lost opportunity to make an easy $5,000—moved to Denver, where she married truck salesman Harlan Lewis in May 1919. They moved to Billings, Montana. For reasons not too hard to guess, Lyda kept this marriage a secret from her friends and relatives. She didn't have to keep the secret long, as she made quick work of husband number three: on June 14, only a month after tying the nuptial knot, Harlan insured himself for $5,000 through the New World Life Insurance Company. Lyda did not neglect to pay the premiums this time. On July 6, he contracted an "illness" of such violence that he had to be strapped to his bed. The doctors thought he died of ptomaine poisoning. They were half right.

Lyda chose to grace Twin Falls again with her presence and relocated there. On August 10, 1919, under the name Anna May McHaffie, she married Edward Meyer at Pocatello. The *very day after the wedding* she insured her groom for a breathtaking (by the standards of the era) $10,000. Edward appears not to have been suspicious of her unseemly haste. They lived on the Perrine Ranch, where he was foreman, at Snake River Canyon, a locale later made notorious when daredevil Evel Knievel attempted to jump across it on a rocket-powered motorcycle in 1974.

But even Mr. Knievel didn't take such chances as the unwitting Edward Meyer, who courted death simply by eating dinner with Lyda on August 25, after fifteen days of marital bliss. He became mortally ill immediately afterward and was rushed to the hospital, where doctors predicted on September 6 that he would make a recovery from his nasty case of "typhoid." But they didn't count on his dutiful wife's insistence on staying by his side. Edward joined the roll call of Lyda's dead on September 7.

This time she had played her winning hand once too often. The suspicious insurance company paid to have Meyer's body scrutinized, and a chemical examination found arsenic. Detectives called Lyda on the carpet and asked her some uncomfortably pointed questions. The investigation had barely begun when the black widow fled to Los Angeles, where she disappeared. Nevertheless, Deputy Sheriff Ormsby ordered that Lyda's daughter, Loraine, and Mr. McHaffie be exhumed and autopsied. Both bodies contained arsenic.

Lyda's activities and whereabouts for the next two years are a mystery, but at some point she married Paul Vincent Southard and ended up in Hawaii, where she was caught in May 1921, as described above. Deputy Sheriff Ormsby took an ocean voyage to retrieve Mrs. Southard and arrived with her in San Francisco on June 7. From there it was a one-way trip to Twin Falls, where she pled not guilty of murdering Edward Meyer. She was permitted to consult with her attorneys without a guard present, as though she had been accused of nothing more serious than plucking a violet in a park. This extraordinary circumstance would be repeated.

Disapprove of Lyda as we might, she certainly had nerve. Although she was about to go on trial for poisoning Meyer, she had the effrontery to file a lawsuit on June 18 against the insurance company because they didn't give her that $10,000 payout!

Her trial began on September 26. Technically, she was tried only for murdering Edward Meyer (husband number four, for the benefit of readers who neglected to fill out a scorecard), but the prosecution sought to introduce details about the miserable demises of husbands one through three, all of whom had developed similar symptoms shortly after being heavily insured. By this time *all* of her victims had been exhumed and examined, and *all* were stuffed to the gills with arsenic. At least one person on planet Earth believed in her innocence: her fifth husband, Mr. Southard, who touchingly supported her at the trial and seemed unaware that she may have been planning to liquidate him for cash at the soonest opportunity.

The prosecution insisted that Lyda get the death penalty. This was probably a tactical mistake, since Idaho had never executed a woman before and was unlikely to start now with a young, charming, and pretty one. The jury deliberated on November 3; the next day they pronounced her guilty—but only of second-degree murder! Yes, a second-degree murder sentence for a woman who had poisoned four husbands, a brother-in-law, and her infant daughter. She was sentenced to a laughable ten years to life in the Old Idaho State Penitentiary. In other words, Lyda conceivably could have been free to perpetrate further matrimonial get-rich-quick schemes by 1931, or sooner if she behaved and got paroled.

On November 26, Paul Southard began divorce proceedings. He must have had second thoughts about the benefits of being married to this woman.

All was silence and stillness from Lyda Southard until May 4, 1931, when she scaled the prison wall with a homemade ladder and escaped with help from an accomplice, a recent parolee named David Minton. She was only thirty-nine years old and attractive enough to continue her mania for serial marriage. And that's exactly what she did: while on the lam she became a housekeeper and cook (!) for Harry Whitlock in Denver and married him on March 10, 1932, after having known him only two months.

Mr. Minton was arrested in Denver on July 1. Realizing the heat was on, Lyda fled Mr. Whitlock's house, oddly without poisoning him first, and was captured in Topeka on July 30. She put up no resistance, telling the officer who arrested her, "I'm Lyda Southard. I expected to be caught." She added ruefully, "I was a fool for having ever left"—whether she meant leaving prison or Mr. Whitlock's residence is a matter for conjecture. Her current husband had some discomfiting moments when he remembered that back in June, his new wife had unsuccessfully tried to sell him on the idea of getting mutual life insurance.

Lyda went back to the Idaho State Pen in August. There was a scandal in 1933 when it was revealed that the warden had been granting Lyda special favors, such as permitting the dangerous black widow, who had already escaped once, to go on unaccompanied visits to town when the whim struck her. A decade later came some good luck for her, though perhaps not for society: she was released on probation on October 3, 1941, and pardoned for good in 1942. She married for a seventh time, to Hal

Shaw of Twin Falls, who vanished several years later. It does not appear that she was suspected of foul play.

Mrs. Lyda Trueblood Dooley McHaffie Lewis Meyer Southard Whitlock Shaw died of a heart attack in Salt Lake City on February 5, 1958. She probably slept soundly at night right up to the very end. She was buried in Twin Falls, the site of so many of her triumphs.

10

MYSTERIOUS MONTANA

An Honest Mistake

In November 1909 a weirdo stole Harfield C.'s son from his grave at Great Falls. Nobody could discern any earthly reason, since the ghoul did not demand ransom, even though Harfield was one of the richest men in the state.

Much later, in May 1911, Harfield received an anonymous note stating that the child's body would be returned if he left $1,500 beside a lantern he would find burning at an isolated section of the Fort Benton road. Harfield saw this as an opportunity to catch the corpse-napper and pretended to follow the letter's demands.

On the night of May 9, Harfield and his brother Arthur dropped a dummy package by a roadside light on the Fort Benton road, as ordered, and drove off in a car. An ex-sheriff named Joseph H. followed on horseback, planning to get the drop on anyone who came for the package. A few miles up the road, the party saw another burning lantern—they had dropped the package at the wrong spot! They drove back to the first site to retrieve it.

As they approached, the brothers saw an armed man stooping over the parcel. They opened fire with results much to the detriment of their friend Mr. H.

Super Skeletons

Prof. Marcus S. Farr of Princeton and several of his students undertook an archaeological dig in the Fish Creek country near Big Timber in July 1903. In addition to primitive tools, fossils (including a mastodon), and a Stone Age city, the expedition unearthed the skeleton of a nine-foot man. He was buried near a woman nearly equal in size. And at the foot of the mound was "the skeleton of an animal that resembled the dog of today, except the animal must have been as large as a small horse."

The Downside of Pioneer Life, Part Two

A rancher who lived twelve miles west of Livingston went insane on August 23, 1890. When the sheriff and his men investigated, they found that the rancher had killed his wife and five children with a broadax. The oldest daughter, age fifteen, was cut nearly in half; all the bodies were mutilated and had their arms and legs cut off. The sheriff and his men found the man of the house sitting in a corner eating a child's arm. When the rancher resisted arrest, one of the men was forced to shoot him in self-defense.

Playing and Slaying

Henry A. and William C.—not mere boys, but adult cowpunchers who should have known better–played a game of "William Tell" at Hardin on September 8, 1922. Henry held out his hat at arm's length and dared William to shoot through it. The latter fired and missed. Henry plunked the hat back on his head and challenged William, who was considered a crack shot, to fire again. William did and was convicted of manslaughter in April 1924. Perhaps because Henry so clearly had played a role in his own demise, the sentence was suspended, and William was let off with a warning, probably something along the lines of "kindly refrain from making targets of hats that perch atop the heads of others."

Ben's Premonition

Pvt. Benjamin Rogers of Madison County, Kentucky, was a twenty-nine-year-old private in Company G, Seventh US Cavalry. (Students of American history may already have some idea where this story is heading.)

The archives of Eastern Kentucky University have a couple of letters Private Rogers sent while stationed in Shreveport, Louisiana, to his cousin J. B. Parkes of Richmond, Kentucky. The first, dated March 15, 1876, is a sometimes comical description of the setbacks in a soldier's life–in Rogers' case, self-inflicted setbacks. All misspellings and eccentricities of grammar are in the original:

> The Seventh is expecting to be ordered to Dakota Territory very soon for the Black Hill Expedition, which will start out next month. They are some talk of our regt. being ordered in Texas to put a stop to the cattle thieves—I can't say which place we will go. If I had any say I would much rather remain here. I have enough of Expeditions in [illegible]. Having but a few months to serve I would like to remain here in Louisiana where it is summer the year round.
>
> Since I written to you I have had a General Court Martial charged with allowing a prisoner while awaiting sentence of Court Martial to escape from me while sentry over him—It was just after pay day, ever body was drunk except the Guard. I went out in charge of the prisoners to have some wood sawed for the Officers' Quarters—During the time one of them escaped from me. I had my belts taken off and was confined in the Guardhouse, general charges preferred—It was a infantry Officer who confined me, preferred the charges against me, was tried by a General. Got ten dollars of my monthly pay stoped for three months, making thirty dollars in all. Three months hard labor in the Guardhouse—You may think that is a very hard sentence but it is not, I was very lucky. Some men would have got twelve months and all their pay for the same period. My company commander done all he could to get me out of it.
>
> It was through him that I got off so light. I was released from confinement and put on parole in the Quartermaster's Department. I have the thirty dollars to pay—then I'll be all right. This is the way they do in the regulars. Soldiers must be very attentive when on duty; if they neglect it any they are severely punished.

The second letter from the Shreveport camp, dated April 17, 1876, is more somber in tone, written after Private Rogers of the Seventh Cavalry got marching orders not to his liking. As Ben makes clear to his cousin Mr. Parkes, his confinement in the guardhouse and wage garnishment now seemed the least of his problems:

> I am very sorry to inform you that I leave tomorrow morning for Dakota Territory. Once more I have to try the wild plains. Rec'd orders from Hd Qrs [headquarters] this morning to leave for Dakota.
>
> To-morrow we depart for that wild country. All the Indians that was on the Reservations have left all on the War Path. As the Seventh have checked them several times, they think in Washington it is useless to send any other Regiment out after them. We were fighting them for two years before we were ordered down here. I have had a very good time for the last year. But now comes for the hard-ships, etc.

Have been in several engagements with them, always came out all right so far. Can not say how I will come out this time. Have never flinched from my duty yet, never will if it takes my life.

Not having but few months to serve, I was in hopes it would expire before being ordered off. We must expect such things when we become soldiers, "obedient to orders." Our Colonel is noted for his Indian fighting, is very fond of the spook [as in spirits?], George A. Custer. . . . Am very little afraid of losing my scalp, though it might be possible. . . . My horse is looking well. So it will take a very fast pony to catch me, provided that I have to retreat.

I'll write just as soon as I arrive off the Expedition. Provided that I get through it safe. If you don't here from me in three or four months you can say that Ben is gone up.

After Rogers' signature, the letter includes a postscript in different handwriting: "Jim—This letter came for you as you see a year ago, but Tom kept it in his pocket until now and I now send it to you. Poor Ben, he seemed to have had a premonition of his doom."

Poor Ben's premonition was right on the money. On June 25, 1876, Private Rogers and 267 other men were massacred by the Sioux and Cheyenne at Little Bighorn. (At the battle Rogers served under Brevet Brig. Gen. Marcus Reno, not the more famous Custer, but both regiments were all part of one large group that got slaughtered.)

Private Rogers lies in a mass grave on Last Stand Hill in Custer National Cemetery, located on the Crow Indian Reservation within Little Bighorn Battlefield, so very far from his beloved home in Madison County, Kentucky.

Vintage Violence: Executions and Lynchings

In the winter of 1882–83, recently paroled convict John Jessrang murdered his friend V. H. Davidson out in the open at Canyon Creek, near Glendale, and then he tried to destroy evidence by cremating the body. The killer unwisely chose to perform these activities during a good old-fashioned Montana blizzard, and his victim's corpse was only partially burned. Karma avenged poor Davidson in spades. Let us examine Jessrang's litany of woe, all of which he could have avoided by leaving Davidson alone:

After he was captured by lawmen, certain masked citizens of Beaverhead County seized him and strung him up five times from the Utah and Northern Railroad's water tank to make him confess.

Officers took him back. He escaped, but his feet were frostbitten, making his recapture simple.

Both of Jessrang's feet were later amputated.

Jessrang was indicted for murder. His case was continued until the next term of court. In the meantime he was stashed in a jail cell in Dillon.

Community feeling was inflamed on March 6, 1883, when what little remained of Davidson's scorched corpus was brought to Glendale. The local paper did not spare details: "A party had visited the scene of the murder and cremation and found, buried in the snow, parts of the body; the hips and lower part of the body and inches of the backbone, the heart and a part of the kidneys were found."

The next week, the law firm representing Jessrang sent him a letter. On March 13, the attorney got his own unopened letter back. Instead of bearing the phrase "return to sender," as one might expect, the envelope had the to-the-point phrase "hanged last night" scrawled on it. This came as news to the attorney, who looked into the matter and found that on March 6, disguised vigilantes had overpowered the jailer and hanged Jessrang in his cell. As if Jessrang's situation were not already bereft of dignity, his pants came off as the mob dragged him across the floor, exposing his bandaged and bloody leg stumps.

But the attorney could at least take solace in his client's bravery when facing the terrors of death: "[He] showed wonderful nerve. Not a complaint or murmur of pain escaped from his pallid lips."

Thomas Salmon was the former president of the Red Lodge Miners' Union in Montana. Superintendent William O'Connor of the Rocky Fork coal mine fired Salmon, and the union activist asserted the rights of the workingman by shooting O'Connor in cold blood. When Salmon was hanged at Red Lodge on January 27, 1899, he refused to have a preacher present, saying, "I want no minister, priest or sky pilot to show me the road to Heaven."

Salmon's last words: "If any of you follow my body to the cemetery, do not uncover your heads and take chances of getting pneumonia. It is a barbarous custom and I hope you will protect yourselves, for by so doing you will please me."

On January 4, 1903, while under the influence of whiskey and morphine, laundryman Louis H. Mott shot his wife, Leah, four times. He was scheduled to hang in Missoula on March 18, 1904. While awaiting his final day, Mott sent a letter to Congressman Joseph Dixon, telling him that his ghost would pay Dixon a visit on March 20. So far as is known, Mott's spirit kept its ethereal yap shut.

Roy Walsh killed a storekeeper in Renova on June 26, 1923. He was hanged in Boulder on February 14, 1925. As the hangman tested the trapdoor, Walsh nonchalantly ate an orange.

From My Cold, Dead Hands

In August 1862, monte dealer and horse thief William B. Arnett was shot by a lawman in a Gold Creek saloon. He happened to be holding his cards in his left hand and his gun in his right. It must have taken the authorities and the undertaker a while to get around to dealing with his body, because by then Arnett's body was in such a state of rigor mortis that neither cards nor weapon could be removed from his death grip. He was buried with them.

Not long afterward, Arnett's partner in crime, C. W. Spillman, was lynched, and Gold Creek became better known as Hangtown. No one had to ask why.

Making Do

In April 1909, an Indian woman living near Port Arthur needed to go fishing to feed her children. The ground was too frozen to procure fishing worms, so she cut off a piece of her own skin to use as bait. Fortunately, the desperate measure was successful.

Spopee Speaks

In spring 1914, a delegation of Sioux visited St. Elizabeths Hospital in Washington, DC. To their surprise, they found an elderly Indian in the ward for the criminally insane whom attendants said had not spoken a single word since his confinement in 1882. The Sioux coaxed him to speak, but the only syllables he uttered sounded like "ba-fo." They interpreted this to mean "Blackfoot."

In May, representatives of the Blackfoot tribe went to the nation's capital to negotiate with the government over reimbursement for land. The Sioux had told them that they thought a member of their tribe was in the asylum, and they checked it out while they were in town.

The Blackfoot delegates—including James Perrine, Charles W. Buck, and Mr. and Mrs. Malcolm Clark—spoke to the elderly, silent, seemingly nearly catatonic Indian in his native tongue to no effect. His visitors tried sign language. The Indian shook his head. But then Mrs. Clark addressed him gently in "little people's talk," the language used by Blackfoot mothers when speaking to their children. She described the native land back in northern Montana; she described rivers, buffalo, bear, and deer.

As though by magic, the elderly man's mental block lifted immediately, and he spoke coherently for the first time in thirty-two years, revealing that his name was Spopee ("Turtle"). This came as a big surprise to the delegates, who had heard stories about the great hunter Spopee when they were children but had assumed he was long dead.

Spopee asked a question: "Where is Three Bears?"

"He died twenty-six years ago," answered a member of the delegation. Spopee did not comprehend the words. The delegate made the tribe's hand signal meaning "death" and counted to twenty-six. Then the elderly man understood.

Three Bears was Spopee's brother.

Word spread quickly through the hospital, and soon Spopee's room was filled with amazed staff including Dr. Glick, who said—as summarized by a *Washington Star* reporter—that they were "witnesses of the most wonderful scene a student of psychology may hope to observe—the return of a human mind, the rebirth of memory, restoration of the coordination of the faculties."

At last the old man told his forgotten story: in 1879, an overzealous army officer waited until the warriors were away from Spopee's village and then attacked, killing women, children, and the elderly, including his mother. The army punished the officer, but this was not good enough for Spopee. He went on the hunt.

While seeking revenge, he found a white fur trader near the Canadian border. One version of events holds that Spopee, assuming the trader was one of the "tribe" that had killed his mother, made quick work of him. On the other hand, Spopee claimed he had killed the trader in self-defense. In any case, soon afterward he was captured by soldiers and taken to stand trial at Fort Benton. The other Blackfoot had no idea what had happened to him after he was escorted away.

In 1880, Spopee was found guilty of murder and got the death penalty. (Later, evidence suggested the killing had taken place in Canada; if so, the case was out of the Montana court's jurisdiction.) His luck turned for the better, sort of: the court sympathized with the fact that he had been retaliating against the massacre of his tribe. His sentence was commuted to life in prison. Spopee misunderstood, thinking that he was going to the "white man's house" (prison) until they put him to death at their convenience. He protested by refusing to speak; in return, his captors thought he had gone insane and had him transferred to the asylum in St. Elizabeths Hospital. And there he stayed, wordless, for more than three decades.

Cato Sells, commissioner of the Bureau of Indian Affairs, asked President Wilson to give Spopee an unconditional pardon. It was granted in July. Before he left, one of the guards at St. Elizabeths paid tribute: "I'll be mighty glad when the old Indian gets his freedom, but I'll be mighty sorry to see him go. In spite of the fact that he never said a word until last Sunday, he's as fine a man as ever lived, and we'll miss him here."

The old hunter returned to Browning, Montana, and to his daughter, Mrs. Mary Takes Gun, who had been a baby when he'd last seen her. The tribe had not forgotten him: Blackfoot mothers had sung a folk song about Spopee to their children for many years.

Five Lynched

Photographer/historian Lambert Florin remarked of Virginia City, Montana, "[It] may well hold the record for mining camp lawlessness and vigilante violence in attempts to control it." This is the kind of thing that gave the town its reputation:

Vigilantes had set their sights on hanging six road agents taking refuge in Virginia City. One, Bill Hunter, had an inkling of what was about to transpire and escaped. The other five were not as nimble in their comprehension or as fast on their feet, and they were captured one by one on January 14, 1864.

First the vigilance committee caught Frank Parrish in a store. He put up no fight and seemed resigned to his fate. Then they arrested "Club Foot George" Lane, then Boone Helm, who none too convincingly declared his innocence. One of the vigilantes, Thomas Dimsdale, later wrote of Helm, "[He] was the most hardened, cool and deliberate scoundrel of the whole band . . . murder was a mere pastime with him. He called repeatedly for whiskey and had to be reprimanded for his unseemly conduct several times." (Helm must have been quite the lively villain. One charge against him was cannibalism—not performed out of grim necessity, Donner Party style, but because he seems to have liked the taste of human meat and snacked on enemies and persons who should have been more discriminating in their choice of companions. He was from Lincoln County, Kentucky, thus his proud nickname: The Kentucky Cannibal.)

After apprehending the gourmandizing Helm, the lynchers rounded up Jack Gallagher in a gambling hall. Their final quarry was Haze Lyons, whom they interrupted as he was about to eat a flapjack in a miner's cabin. His captors offered to let him finish his meal, but Lyons put down his fork, remarking, "I lost my appetite."

Most men in the Wild West who had the distinction of being lynched met their fate under a tree limb. The vigilantes were in a hurry to finish their business at hand before the bandits' friends attempted to rescue them, so they led the five to an unfinished building at Wallace Street and Van Buren. There was no privacy, however. Since the structure was not completely built, a huge crowd could see clearly the activities within.

Five ropes were thrown around a ceiling beam; five boxes were placed side by side. The outlaws were ordered to stand on the boxes, and then the ropes were fastened around their necks.

Jack Gallagher cried. He asked for and was granted a slug of Valley Tan whiskey, which fueled his bravado. "How do I look in this necktie, boys?" he jollied his ill-fated friends.

Boone Helm was disgusted with Gallagher's bouts of weeping. "Stop making such a fuss," the Kentucky Cannibal admonished. "There's no use being afraid to die." Indeed, Helm complained more about his sore finger than his impending death.

George Lane, apparently unable to bear the suspense or perhaps wishing to deny his captors some pleasure, jumped off his box of his own volition. "There's one gone to hell," observed Helm, who then shouted, "Every man for his own principles! Hurrah for Jeff Davis! Let her rip!"

The vigilance committee kicked away the boxes, and the highwaymen strangled to death, condemned without benefit of a trial. Their bodies were laid in a row in the street for their friends to collect. They were buried in a line in the cemetery on a hill above town. The outlaws didn't even get the dignity of grave markers, at least not at first.

Sometime later there was a debate among the lynchers as to the exact location of their victims' burial spots. Two of them went to the hill and dug until they found the decomposed remains of Club Foot George Lane, identifiable by his distinctive namesake. The road agents were reburied under five wooden markers—with the exception of Lane's club foot, which was put on display first in a saloon and later in a museum. The rope-burned hanging beam and Virginia City's Boot Hill still exist and await the tourist.

As for Bill Hunter, the criminal who had skipped town just before the lynching party, he was hanged by vigilantes at Gallatin Valley on February 3, having extended his lifespan two whole weeks by fleeing.

Domestic Delusion

Joseph M. of St. Paul left for Yellowstone Park on April 28, 1896, to start a new job at the Mammoth Hot Springs Hotel. "The change in the climate did not agree with him," explained a hometown paper, the *St. Paul Globe*, "and the day after his arrival he complained about it." He must have *really* hated the weather; on April 30, only two days after his arrival, "He went out for a walk, and either lost his way or was overcome," in the words of the *Globe*. The newspaper diplomatically did not mention that he got drunk as a boiled owl before stepping out into the bitterly cold night. He did not return.

His body was found on May 11, frozen like Jack Nicholson in the last reel of *The Shining*. Splinters of aspen between Joseph's teeth indicated that he had been reduced to eating tree bark in his final hours. Strangely, before dying of exposure he had removed his coat and vest, and his body was found reclining on a log. Wrote Lee Whittlesey in *Death in Yellowstone*, "In his dementia he had apparently believed himself at home safe in bed."

The Wrong Sausage!

William V. did three stupid things in rapid succession in his Missoula home on December 10, 1912. The first was that he decided to rid himself of a dog by stuffing a sausage with strychnine. The second was that he put the tainted sausage back on the plate with the *other* sausages. The third was that he absentmindedly helped himself.

The dog hater spent a very interesting solitary twelve hours before he was found. His last words: "I must have gotten hold of the wrong one."

How Helpful

John F., a sixty-four-year-old miner at Clancy, was nothing if not detail-oriented. On May 7, 1891, he dug his own grave in a hillside and placed his homemade pine casket beside it. Then he walked to his cabin on Strawberry Creek, placed the barrel of a rifle over his heart, and pulled the trigger with a stove poker. He left a note explaining that he didn't want to cause anyone inconvenience: "I don't want to trouble anybody. Bury me in the coffin I built and in the grave I dug."

The End of a Running Joke

Mr. Wheeler, a member of the 25th Regiment Band at Fort Missoula, shared a strange sense of humor with his friend Charley F., owner of a saloon. The barkeep kept a loaded shotgun in his establishment, and whenever Wheeler and Charley happened to meet, one would aim the gun at the other and jestingly threaten to shoot. On October 16, 1888, Wheeler sauntered by the saloon, and Charley invited him in. When Wheeler entered, Charley commenced their customary routine, expecting the usual boffo laffs. But this time . . .

Why It Doesn't Pay to Have Large Hands

Arthur F. Hughes of Forsyth was involved in a plot to make lots of money fast: insure his own life to the tune of $8,000; burn down his ranch house with a body inside; hide out for a while in a distant place under a pseudonym; let his wife collect the payment; return later and share the bounty. Couldn't be easier!

One obvious difficulty was that Arthur required a body to use as a stand-in, and he couldn't exactly purchase a corpse at Cadavers-R-Us. His solution was to rob the grave of Mr. Craig, a recently deceased neighbor.

On March 6, 1913, all was good to go. Hughes, his wife, Sarah, and their confederate—a farmhand named Rice—exhumed Craig's body and placed it in the house. They set a fire, Mr. Hughes scurried off to New York City to become a longshoreman, and a grieving Mrs. Hughes got a fat check from the Montana Life Insurance Company.

Then an unexpected complication arose: love, sweet love! A month after the swindle, Sarah Hughes fell for farmhand Rice and married him, making the fake widow a genuine bigamist. Then there was another complication of the sort that usually unravels these would-be diabolically clever schemes: Montana authorities believed at first that the charred remains were those of Mr. Hughes, but an autopsy showed no smoke in the dead man's lungs, so they revised their opinion and thought he had been murdered. Rice and his new bride were arrested and placed in the Rosebud County jail.

Mr. Hughes heard about the romance, and in October he sent his wife a letter complaining bitterly about her brief mourning period. The note went straight to the jail, of course, and the sheriff read it with great interest, considering that its author was supposed to be dead.

The NYPD arrested Hughes in a Park Row saloon—they identified him by his freakishly large hands—and held him until he could be extradited to Montana on charges of arson, grand larceny, and grave robbery.

It was the last charge that really troubled him, as he thought Montanans would take it most seriously. "They'll lynch me if they ever get me in that jail out there for grave robbery," he plaintively fretted. He didn't even get any of the $8,000.

11

CREEPY COLORADO

Extraordinary Epitaph

Inscribed on a boulder near Mt. Pisgah Church, Cripple Creek: "He called Bill Smith a liar."

Bizarre Bequests

Former deputy district attorney J.E.K. of Boulder killed his wife and himself on January 27, 1929. He left the following items in his will: "Unto those who have sought to double-cross, to condemn, to criticize unjustly and bear false witness, I leave my revenge implanted within their own consciences, and may it ever be a spur and pointed sword therein, that similar wrongs be not imposed on others."

At the same time, "Forgiveness personally, of course, is bequeathed to all . . ."

To the children of Boulder, J.K. bequeathed the "sunshine and fresh air, the music of the birds and the bees," things that really weren't his to give away. Very poetic, but I bet they'd have preferred money.

George D., a Denver rag picker, wanted his funeral to be held in the barroom of the Windsor Hotel and for his pallbearers to toast his memory with a good snort of whiskey to the accompaniment of his favorite song, "It's Springtime in the Rockies." These pretty rituals were performed on

December 14, 1935. In addition, George—an amateur mathematician—requested that each mourner enter a number on an adding machine near his casket. The sum of the numbers would be "a message to the High Celestial Mathematician" to allow his soul into heaven. You might say George was a little eccentric.

In a Pickle

The abandoned cemetery at Glenwood Springs had long since been replaced by a newer graveyard. The city was expanding in size, so progress dictated that the thirty or so pioneers in the old cemetery would have to be exhumed and relocated to the new burying ground in January 1892. The sexton in charge was surprised to find that so many of the unearthed coffins were in mint condition. He opened one casket "out of mere curiosity" and found the cadaver within as well-preserved as its container: "The body was not shrunken or in any way changed apparently, from what it was when first buried but, on the contrary, the flesh was soft and the limbs pliable and the features as natural as life." (That means the curious sexton must have *felt* the long-buried body too.) All of the other corpses were also delightfully fresh. It was assumed that the high lime content in the cemetery's soil acted as a preservative.

Body Snatching: The Ultimate Dirty Job

In the last week of April 1889, the widow of Col. J. A. G. of Denver was informed that her husband's body had been unearthed from his grave, and she could get it back if she paid several thousand dollars. Instead she called in detectives, who quickly solved the crime and arrested five citizens, one of whom was a woman and another a prominent grocer. The body snatchers had written up a secret agreement among themselves vowing secrecy and promising death to any member of the gang who spilled the beans. All signed it—but one was dumb enough to carry the document on his person, where it was found when detectives searched him. The colonel was uncovered from his hiding place in the prairie three miles from the cemetery on May 2.

A Slight Misdiagnosis

In spring 1881, Christopher S. was found dead in bed at Pueblo. The coroner and the doctors examined the body, determined that he had died of diphtheria, and buried him. In November Christopher's body was exhumed and sent east. There it was examined a second time, and doctors found a bullet hole in the back of the head. The murderer—a real craftsman!—had sealed the wound with a wooden plug so expertly as to make his handiwork nearly undetectable.

Death Diary

An avalanche in December 1908 covered fifty-six-year-old Samuel F.'s cabin at Lime Creek, fourteen miles east of Silverton. So deep were the drifts that Samuel's body wasn't recovered until May 1909. He had kept a diary as he'd slowly perished over the course of three weeks from illness and starvation:

> December 13—Taken suddenly ill; in great pain.
> December 15—Am getting worse.
> December 18—Snowslide covered cabin today.
> December 25—Christmas day; too weak to dig out of slide; can't get to town.
> January 1—I believe I am dying.
> January 2—Too weak to get up.
> January 3—I—
> January 4—I can—
> January 5—[Illegible scrawl.]

Samuel's gravestone in San Juan Cemetery, Silverton, memorializes him as "The Hermit of Lime Creek."

Chain Reaction

Seven-year-old Charles M. of Pueblo got a set of ice skates for Christmas 1935. While trying them out for the first time on December 26, he fell through thin ice and drowned in Fountain River.

Mrs. Helen D. tried to resuscitate Charles, contracted pneumonia, and died on December 31. A few days later, on January 3, 1936, her husband, John, died from shock following her death.

A Light at His Feet

In 1884, a prominent citizen and pioneer known only as James told this strange story to a *Denver News* reporter.

James had grown up in central Illinois but moved to Colorado to seek his fortune in the mines at Russell Gulch. In June 1870, he was overcome with such a strong urge to visit his father and brother that he made the journey home to Illinois despite the great inconvenience.

After traveling for several days, James arrived at a train station five miles from his father's house. No one knew of his arrival, so he had to walk all the way home through a forest—in the rain—at night. Soon James lost the trail and wandered aimlessly. He was apprehensive, with good reason: he remembered the terrain well enough to know that the Sangamon River ran on one side of the path, and somewhere there was a high bluff with sharp and jagged rocks at the bottom. It was nearby—but where?

James picked his way through the blackness for about two miles when he realized that someone he could not clearly see was walking beside him. Then James saw that "a strange, supernatural sort of light was burning at my feet as I walked, illuminating my path; by its light I discovered to my horror that I was on the very brink of the precipice." After backing away in terror, James saw his companion: a man in a gray suit with a red handkerchief covering the lower part of his face in the style of a Western bandit. Despite his disquieting appearance, James was drawn to him instinctively, as though to an old friend. He wasn't even frightened when it dawned on him that the man seemed to be a ghost. "That was a mighty narrow escape," James said to the man, who nodded silently.

The rain stopped. James continued his walk home accompanied by his quiet friend and the strange glow at his feet. Eventually he made it to his father's lawn; the window was illuminated. Turning, James saw that both the man and the ghostly light were gone.

When James entered the house, he found his father in a deep depression because his other son had vanished. The old man explained, "Ten days ago he left home with a considerable sum of money, the returns for the last year's crop which we had just sold, intending to deposit it in the bank in town." But he'd never made it to the bank, and he'd never come home.

A strange feeling came over James. "What did he wear when he left home?" he asked.

"A gray suit and a red handkerchief."

In the morning James and his father retraced the journey of the night before. They found the body of James's brother lying in a creek—wearing a gray suit adorned with a red handkerchief. An examination of the body showed that he had been bashed in the head and was penniless, a highwayman's victim.

James persuaded his father to sell his business and farm. They took the proceeds and bought a nice house on Capitol Hill in Denver.

Vintage Violence: Executions and Lynchings

William Coe and his gang robbed citizens and rustled cattle in Oklahoma, New Mexico, and Colorado in the years just after the Civil War. The US

Cavalry finally caught Coe in Madison, NM, and he was taken to the jail in Pueblo, Colorado. But Pueblo's Vigilance Committee decided Coe would make a nice feather in their cap, and they stole him from his cell on the night of July 20, 1868. They were unusually subtle for a lynch mob—they hanged Coe in secret and hid his body. His disappearance was considered a mystery for years until his skeleton was discovered. It still wore manacles and leg irons, which helped nail down its identity.

A true tale of frontier mayhem and its grim aftermath was enacted in Lake City when Sheriff Edward N. Campbell suspected two Bluff Street saloonkeepers, George Betts and James Browning, of moonlighting as burglars. Late on the night of April 27, 1882, W. G. Luckett's house was broken into, but many valuables were left behind. The sheriff had an idea that the thieves might be greedy enough to return and collect the rest of it, so he and his deputies hid and waited.

After a while they heard someone trying to break in through the door. "Throw up your hands!" commanded the sheriff. But giving the burglars advance warning was a fatal error. They fired in the darkness, killing Campbell.

A posse pursued Betts and Browning, caught them at dawn, and brought them back to the Lake City jail. If the killers spent the day worrying about their necks, they had good reason. When night fell, crowds of hooded miners approached the jail carrying ominous impedimenta such as rifles, shotguns, a sledgehammer, and ropes. A hundred other citizens didn't even trouble to disguise themselves. The prisoners were carried to Ocean Wave Bridge (now called the Ball Flats Bridge) and summarily hanged.

Many years later, an elderly man who had been a child in Lake City at the time related to historian Muriel Wolle that the morning after the lynching, the schoolmaster had given the children an object lesson in obeying the law: he had trooped the kids down to the bridge to see Betts and Browning, still swaying in the gentle breeze like sunflowers. It was the sort of homily neglected by their *McGuffey Readers*.

I must not neglect to mention in passing that Lake City was near the place where, in winter 1874, Alferd Packer immortalized himself in American history when he decided the five men he was prospecting with would make better snacks than traveling companions. How many communities can claim lynching and cannibalism as part of their heritage?

Rose M. was a ten-year-old girl who lived with Mr. and Mrs. Mike C. of Ouray. It was a good deal for the guardians but not so much for Rose, who was worked like a mule and beaten like one as well.

On January 12, 1884, a hunter found Rose unconscious beside a haystack. He alerted Mr. C., who took the child home. She died a few hours later, and Mr. C. buried her without informing anyone. Nothing suspicious about that!

Word got out, and on January 16 the coroner ordered the body exhumed. He discovered signs of recent severe mistreatment, including bruises, scars, and stab wounds. Mr. and Mrs. C. were arrested, along with C.'s brother-in-law, and held in the Delmonico Hotel.

The overwork, abuse, and murder of a little girl did not sit well with the locals, and on the night of January 18 a mob carried the prisoners from the Delmonico. The vigilantes let the brother-in-law go when they decided that he knew nothing of the murder. As for the married couple, however, they were hauled to the town limits and, according to a press account, hanged "quietly and neatly," Mrs. C. from the ridgepole of a house and her husband from a tree across the road. Mrs. C. became the first woman to be lynched in Colorado, which is a distinction of some sort.

On February 12, 1886, two miners at Red Cliff—Mike Gleason and a man named Perry—got into an argument over five bucks that the latter owed the former. Perry shot Gleason in the heart and was taken to jail. On February 14, two hundred miners celebrated Valentine's Day by procuring a rope, overpowering the sheriff, and dragging Perry to a railroad water tank they intended to use as a makeshift gallows. Perry requested that the crowd allow him to jump so he could enjoy the luxury of a quick and painless neck breaking, but the miners wanted to see him strangle. They secured the noose around Perry's neck and pulled him upward. Perry used his last precious breath to curse the mob.

A prisoner named Reynolds escaped from the penitentiary after stabbing a guard to death. He was captured by Cañon City lawmen on January 26, 1900, but immediately afterward was plucked from their hands by a mob and summarily executed. The hanging was distinguished from other events of its kind by an odd feature: after Reynolds was re-arrested, all the fire bells in town were rung as a prearranged signal for residents who wanted to see the lynching. Nearly all of them did, of course.

Sheepmen and cattlemen were at war in Routt County at the turn of the last century, resulting in Bert C., a well-known cattle rancher, being hanged from a tree limb at Slater. His lynchers pinned a curious note to his coat: "You may look all you want to, but don't make any inquiries." His body was found on or around August 1, 1900.

Someone blew up the buildings of the Sun and Moon Mine at Idaho Springs in late July 1903, and citizens were determined to make an example of the culprits. So they went to the jail, took fourteen prisoners away from the sheriff, and—horsewhipped them in the streets? Lynched them? No, they simply marched them to the town limits and ordered the suspects to leave and never come back. The mob even collected money for the poorer prisoners' traveling expenses. True, they were run out of town without a trial, but certainly it was better than being hanged.

Eighteen-year-old Walter Reppin was sentenced to die in Colorado's gas chamber for murdering a taxi driver. Another Walter—specifically, tuberculosis victim Walter D. of Colorado Springs—wrote to the governor requesting that he be executed in Reppin's stead. Since he was dying anyway, why not?

Reppin had made a confession and been declared sane. He admitted he had planned to form a "crime club" to prey on society. This was the sort of fellow Walter D. believed should dodge the chair and be set free. Not surprisingly, Colorado's prison authorities thought Walter D.'s plan lacked common sense and refused his generous offer.

Reppin's sentence was commuted to life imprisonment in October 1934.

Death row isn't usually a place where people have a good time, but Leonard Lee Belongia and brothers Louis and John Pacheco did their best. The Pachecos were scheduled to go to Colorado's gas chamber in Canon City on May 31, 1935; Belongia was slated to meet the same fate on June 21. But the brothers made such friends with Belongia that the latter wrote to Governor Edwin C. Johnson, imploring him to change his execution date because he wanted to die with his prison pals. He pointed out that the death chamber had three seats, so it could accommodate them all quite easily.

"I want the governor to let me go with them," urged Belongia, "because I have been the happiest of my entire life here in the death house and cannot bear to think of watching them go away."

Not surprisingly, the governor denied the request. The Pachecos went to the gas chamber on schedule, with a stoicism that should serve as an example to today's youth.

Belongia—who had murdered rancher Albert Oesterick on December 16, 1934—was unworried about his imminent fate. In addition, unlike many death row inmates, he was convinced that he richly deserved his punishment. He said to Warden Roy Best:

> I believe I am going to get more fun out of this little party than you are. I look at it this way. I have spent eight solid years of my twenty-four years in prison. I serve a term, I get out, go straight awhile and then something snaps and I pull a crime. I owe something to the world and that is my death. I reason it this way: suppose they gave me a life sentence. That means in fifteen years maybe I would be free again. I would go straight a year or two and then the unexplainable would happen and the crime would be more heinous than this one because my crime record is a progression in degree, each worse than the last.

On the night of his execution, Belongia held a light so Warden Best could read the death warrant to him. "All set, warden, I'm ready to go," said Belongia. "Lead me to it. I've had a swell time here and I'm not anxious to get rid of these swell fellows. The warden has treated me wonderfully."

The condemned man walked to the gas chamber in a cheery mood, jesting and smoking a cigar. He said to the attending priest, "Father, if you will smile through this thing, I will too."

Belongia offered his body to the University of Denver for scientific research. The university accepted. He left behind a second legacy: a letter addressed to parents in general, condemning orphanages and warning of the downfalls of punishing children too harshly.

A blind man asked the warden at Colorado State Prison if he could attend the gas chamber executions of Pete Catalina and Angelo Agnes on September 29, 1939. The would-be witness explained that he wanted to discover whether he could "sense death" without seeing it. The warden turned down the ghoulish request.

An Indian Lynching

The trouble began in June 1891 when a Chinese immigrant, Ah Quong Tia, clubbed a Piute Indian called Poker Tom—in self-defense, he swore. Afterward he cut Tom's body into pieces to escape detection. Tom's tribesmen believed a rumor that Ah Quong fricasseed Tom's head and served his heart at a banquet.

Ah Quong surrendered to the police on June 8 and went on trial in Bridgeport the next day. It was no secret that the Piute intended to lynch the "Chinaman" if he were acquitted. Nevertheless, the justice of the peace found him not guilty and left him to fend for himself. Immediately, a couple hundred Indians dragged Ah Quong from the courtroom, bound him, and led him a half mile from town. They lynched him in this subtle and understated fashion:

1. Poker Tom's brother amputated Ah Quong's arm.
2. Then the Indians cut off his other arm.
3. They opened Ah Quong's chest with a cleaver.
4. They festooned the sagebrush with his innards.

"The butchery was witnessed by two white men," noted the press. Nobody interfered, not even the sheriff. The Chinese consulate in San Francisco expressed concern over the matter, but no one else did.

The Mysterious Denver Strangler

Denver is famous for many things, but it hasn't received credit for being home to one of America's earliest (and most obscure) serial killers—an uncaught, unidentified murderer the city's press called "Denver's Jack the Ripper."

Like England's Jack, the Denver man sought his prey among prostitutes. His first victim, so far as is known, was Lena Tapper, strangled in bed in her Market Street home on September 3, 1889.

The next victim was also murdered on Market Street. She was Marie Contassoit (or Contassot) of France, age twenty-three, strangled on October 28. A rope was found nearby; Marie's face was purple and her eyes bulged. Yet the coroner at first declared the cause of death "unknown." Marie got a decent burial in Riverside Cemetery, an unusual circumstance for one of her profession.

The newspapers called the area "Strangler's Row." Perhaps the publicity made the killer restrain himself, since things were quiet for a few years. Then a twenty-four-year-old Japanese prostitute named Kiku Oyama was strangled at 170 Market Street on November 13, 1894. As with the other women, the killer manually strangled her into unconsciousness and afterward finished his work with a towel wrapped tightly around her throat. In each case, the towel was stuffed in the victim's mouth postmortem. Oyama had lived in Denver for only a year.

Suspects were arrested, questioned, investigated, and finally released: a Frenchman named Charles Chaloup, allegedly Contassoit's pimp; Tony Saunders, said to be Contassoit's boyfriend; in January 1895, two more Frenchmen, Alphonse Lamar and Victor Monchereaux; Imi Oyama, a Japanese man who had lived with Kiku while falsely pretending to be her husband.

One of the most promising suspects was Richard Demady, who lived with Lena Tapper, the first victim. After her death he sent a letter to the second victim asking her to live with him. She turned down his generous offer and was herself strangled within weeks. Demady went to trial for killing Lena Tapper but was acquitted on May 10, 1895.

No more prostitute stranglings occurred in Denver after Oyama's death, with the possible exception of twenty-year-old Mabel Brown, murdered in a Market Street house on July 6, 1903. The press noted, "The case in many of its details strongly suggested the series of murders by strangulation which took place in this neighborhood some years ago."

But there also was a creepy, *X-Files*–like incident associated with the series of crimes: Mrs. Julius Voght, a self-professed psychic, lived on Champa Street. She told the police that spirits had given her a description of the murderer while she was in a trance. On October 7, 1898, she was found lying facedown in her apartment—strangled with a towel. Police thought her killer may well have been the Denver Strangler. Perhaps he believed in ghosts and thought he'd better remove the clairvoyant before she gave away his identity.

A Famished Phantom

Philip P., a seventy-three-year-old retired railroad auditor, was bludgeoned to death in his home at 3335 West Moncrieff Place, Denver, on October 17, 1941. Mrs. P., who had spent several months in the hospital before and after her husband's murder, returned to the house to live the sad life of a widow.

But not for very long. Both she and the housekeeper, Edith C., heard strange noises in the night. Household objects had a habit of disappearing.

An unnerved Mrs. P. abandoned the place and moved in with her son; Edith quit, convinced there was a ghost about. She even saw a man's hand and foot in the doorway at the bottom of the stairs that led from the kitchen to the second floor.

Neighbors agreed that the place was haunted because they heard noises issuing from the house and saw unexplained lights late at night. After ten months of being spooked, neighbors insisted that the police investigate the murder house.

On July 30, 1942, investigators did a thorough search, even checking the unventilated, windowless attic. And there they found the "ghost"—Theodore Edward C., age fifty-nine, emaciated, shaggy-haired, and starving, and the admitted murderer of Philip P. The attic stank so badly from the heat and Theodore's accumulated filth that a detective fainted after sniffing its mephitic air, which a reporter likened to a "breath from hell." The hole leading to the attic was so tiny, they marveled that a full-grown man could squeeze through it.

Theodore explained that in September 1941 he had broken into the house while the owners were away and thought the attic a warm, snug place for a homeless drifter such as himself to hide. (Theodore had been acquainted with Mr. and Mrs. P. some thirty years before and only recently returned to the area.) He would creep from his hiding place at night while the couple was asleep. He shaved with Mr. P's razor whenever the man of the house was away.

On the night of October 17, 1941, however, Mr. P. caught him filching a roast. Theodore killed the elderly gentleman in a panic and retreated to the attic—and there he stayed until found. He decorated the place with an old crystal set radio, an electric hot plate, and bedding, all stolen from his victim. After Mrs. P. vacated the house, he sneaked out at night and stole food from stores and other houses, returning to his hideaway before dawn.

Theodore was sentenced to life in the Colorado State Penitentiary, and there he died on May 16, 1967. The press had long ago nicknamed him "the Spider Man."

From the Other Half to the White Hibiscus

Judson D. hailed from Denver. He lived at 128 East Bayaud Avenue and served in the Colorado National Guard during the Great War. He enrolled at Colorado Agricultural College in 1919 and specialized in dairy production. There in Denver his first wife, Mabel, divorced him on August 9, 1927, on charges of adultery and cruelty. He "physically associated with other women" (that was the adultery) and was so caddish as to boast openly about it (that was the cruelty). This circumstance was to be freighted with a certain irony a few years later, when Judson achieved a measure of national notoriety.

By the early 1930s, Judson had moved to San Leandro, California, where he became the city's official milk inspector. Judson, age thirty-four, was aware that his younger second wife, Helen, had struck up a friendship with a twenty-three-year-old University of California, Berkeley student and aspiring poet named Lamar H.

Judson had no problem with the relationship until June 1934, when he found lovestruck letters and poems from Lamar to Helen, whose own verse had been published under the pseudonym "Helen Joy."

On July 26, Judson confronted Lamar with the letters at a ranch near Woodland, where the student had a summer job. Judson demanded that Lamar hand over his wife's letters. He also commanded Lamar to admit his attraction to Helen was only physical and that he write a note to her formally ending the relationship. The young poet refused; his distinctly unpoetic rejoinder was "go to hell!" Judson later said that at that moment "everything went blank," and when he came to his senses Lamar was on the bunkhouse floor with a bullet in his stomach. He died hours later on the operating table.

The *Denver Post* was so impressed by the sudden fame of its native son that in one issue it dedicated two stories to the shooting.

To show he was a good sport, Judson sent flowers to Lamar's funeral. "I have nothing against the boy," he said. "In many ways he was a nice lad." Helen also seemed pretty nonchalant about the recent events. "No matter what happened, or may happen, I love Judson and shall stand by him," she said. "He has forgiven me and all we ask is a chance to start over again."

Of course, the authorities were not going to let it go at that, and Judson went on trial for murder at the end of October. His defense was based on the "unwritten law"—the concept that murder was justified if committed against a homewrecker. (See the section on Utah's Bradley-Brown shooting for more on this legal dodge that, in times past, helped many a murderer walk the streets free and joyful.)

If nothing else, Judson's trial offers a valuable life lesson to overheated young writers and smitten poets: anything you record on paper during your amorous agonies may become a matter of public record someday, and if you aren't dead, you will wish you were. Lamar H.'s mushy letters to Mrs. D. were read aloud in court. He called her his "white hibiscus," and that was just for starters. He referred to her as "my lovely bride" and "sweet one" and often lapsed into the incoherence that only love or breathing paint thinner fumes can inspire.

One letter included the lines "Oh, I love, Helen Louise. I am feeling the pangs of our separation. There is much I would tell you if you were close."

Another one: "Helen, dear, you are my other half always. You are the white core of this spire burning in my heart. Forever and a day with mountains of years on my head."

And another: "If I can help you in your quest, my soul will go with it. If I can help you in your explorations to unknown parts of yourself, I will."

And: "There is a young bride and young groom here [at the ranch where Lamar worked] to be photographed. How beautiful, how tremulous, how rich the air is with fragrance of the gardenias. They have chosen the road of life together and society sanctions them the right of the way on that road."

Also: "Oh, Helen, dearest one, promise me you won't get thinner. Oh, you must put on weight even if it means the isolation of my desires. . . . Be happy with Judson, for what am I but a pale shadow, a seed pearl, a symbol of what is to come. Oh I love you. I press you to close to my heart forever and a day." (For some reason he signed that one, and several others, "Lamar and Lamar.")

Furthermore: "Not even the great mountain of blood in a whale surging to his mate and through her . . . can compare with my love with you. My lips and yours and you thrilling me forever."

Here's how simply *getting a note* from Helen affected Lamar: "Trembling, I opened it. Each red petal against the white pages where your pencil had gone thrilled me. . . . Blue water that slips across the gray stone runs over your shoulders and breast. You are there with each tall pine, like green hope above your hair—your dark hair flows by lilac-scented winds and lies across my face."

Bloody whales and watery breasts aside, Lamar had his down-to-earth moments too. In several of his love letters, he paused during his feverish effusions to complain about the mosquitoes. In one he thanked Helen for keeping him supplied with postage stamps: "I thank you dearly for the stamps." And in another, Lamar put aside the poetry and got practical, suggesting that he and Helen run off to Mexico together. Helen's letters to Lamar were equally tropical and larded with obscure imagery. Naturally, the newspapers couldn't get enough of this stuff.

Lamar vowed in one message to Helen that he would die for her, as indeed he did. When Judson took the stand on November 5, he insisted that he had every right to shoot the person who was trying to drive a wedge between himself and his wife. It was a point of honor, he said.

Judson contended that all he wanted was for Lamar to stop courting his wife. But if this were the case, why did he bring a gun to their meeting at the ranch? The prosecution argued that this indicated premeditation. The youthful poet's dying words were related by his brother Paul: "[Judson] asked me to write a statement saying all I wanted was her body. I said, 'It's not true, but I'll write it—but I'd rather be shot!' Then [he] shot me."

The prosecution wanted Mrs. D. to testify in court. No doubt she would have had many interesting things to say, but the White Hibiscus made herself scarce, and they were unable to subpoena her.

The case went to the jury. They quarreled so loudly in the deliberating room that people outside could hear. After thirty hours of arguing, the jury was hopelessly hung, with seven in favor of acquittal and five in favor of sending Judson to prison. No one believed Judson should go to the hangman. The jury was dismissed on November 9.

Judson's second trial commenced in December 1934. The judge instructed the jury to consider that the law provides plenty of nonviolent opportunities for a wronged spouse to gain redress. Disregarding the judge's hint, this jury came to a decision after nineteen hours: they felt Judson had every right under the unwritten law to shoot the man who had tried to steal his wife, and he was acquitted. That the jury was composed of eleven men and one woman might have had some bearing on their decision. The verdict was greeted with rousing cheers, but none came from the dead poet's mother, who fumed, "He's guilty of murdering my son and nothing can change it. Nothing ever will. He ought to be hanged. There's nothing behind this verdict but sentiment. We're not through with [him] yet."

In fact, the legal system itself wasn't through with Judson D. yet. Even before the murder charge was filed against him, the city of San Leandro performed an investigation indicating Judson had embezzled $1,800 in city funds. At his trial for *this* crime, he pled guilty to stealing a measly $16.93. But San Leandro took that $16.93 seriously, and in March 1935 Judson was sentenced to one to ten years in San Quentin.

The hot-tempered Denver native was paroled on May 12, 1938. He said he was going to move to Lodi, where his wife, Helen, faithfully awaited him, her head turned no longer by lovelorn amateur poets who thought her dark hair flowed in lilac-scented winds.

Culture Clash

Soon after Platt N.'s wife, Molly, died, he wrapped their seventeen-day-old daughter in a blanket and buried her alive with her mother. His father-in-law had demanded he do so.

Sounds like an open-and-shut murder case, but there were complicating legal factors: Platt was a member of the Ute tribe in southwestern Colorado; his father-in-law was Mormon Joe, the medicine man; and the live inhumation of the child was a tribal ritual. And it wasn't the pre-Columbian era or even the days of the Wild West. It was February 1925.

The deputy superintendent of the reservation got wind of the burial, and on March 31 Platt was held pending an investigation. The next day, a US marshal from Denver arrested Platt for murder and his father-in-law for being an accessory. They were clapped in the jail at Cortez. On his very first day in stir, Mormon Joe beat a Mexican cellmate to death with a table leg for daring to question the propriety of burying an infant alive.

Platt went on trial in Pueblo on November 8. He explained that he had loved his wife very much, had been brokenhearted when she'd died, and had believed that she would return to life if he buried their child with her. His defense was that he simply did what the medicine man told him. In fact, he was afraid not to: the medicine man's word was law, and Platt worried that he might be killed himself if he failed to comply. Considering what Mormon Joe had done to his cellmate, Platt may have been correct.

Here was a culture clash indeed. What Platt did was acceptable according to the ancient customs of his tribe but illegal by United States law. Which way of life would prevail? The answer came on November 16: Platt was acquitted on a technicality, which means the authorities got to dodge a difficult legal question. As for Mormon Joe, two days after killing his cellmate in a rage, he was sentenced to twenty-five to thirty years in jail.

Murder Most Fowl

Elderly DeWitt J. and wife Belle of Hutchinson, Kansas, moved into a room on the second floor of the Bonaventure Hotel in Denver, in June 1912. Mrs. J. was noted for criticizing her husband in a louder tone of voice than seemed necessary, both inside and outside their room. One of her sweet pet names for him was "You Old Bum." They were last seen alive on December 7, 1912. Three days later they were found dead in their room, each with a bullet in the head. Mrs. J. was in bed, and her husband was stretched across the foot of the same with a revolver clenched in his hand. The papers helpfully noted that Mrs. J.'s face and upper half were bloated and decomposing, but Mr. J. was sound as a dollar; he had swallowed carbolic acid before shooting himself, and the substance worked as a preservative. It seemed an open-and-shut case of murder and suicide, but police wondered: Was there a way to be sure?

As it turned out, there was a potential witness, sort of: the couple's parrot, Susie, had been found walking up and down on the bed's footboard, muttering, "Here, here, here" at the bodies. Detectives' eyes brightened. What if the parrot had overheard the last words discussed by its owners? Could it be encouraged to speak? Then they could *know* what really happened! On December 13 they called in a bird expert, who was unable to coax a word from the parrot. The detectives spent the night huddled around the bird's cloth-covered cage, hoping that if it thought it was alone, it might soliloquize in its shrill, soulless voice. No such luck. The case was classified as a domestic murder-suicide, and the authorities were left looking rather silly. But at least Susie got her picture in the *Denver Post*.

The Second Item of Business

Leadville was founded in 1877 and incorporated on February 18, 1878. The city fathers' main concerns on that festive occasion tell us something about the priorities of our frontier ancestors. After six hundred citizens gathered in a gambling hall, their first major issue was to officially name the town. The second item of pressing business was from the Vigilance Committee, which reported purchasing a supple new rope that they had just used to lynch a claim jumper.

The Grave That Wasn't

At one time, travelers who visited Pike's Peak could see a cairn resembling a grave with a wooden board reading "Erected in memory of Erin O'Keefe, daughter of John and Nora O'Keefe, who was eaten by mountain rats in the year 1876." In fact, the grave became a tourist attraction, and few who visited the peak left without being photographed beside the bizarre inscription, because that's the kind of thing that makes good vacation memories.

Few knew that the grave was an utter sham. In 1876, an Eastern newspaper published a hoax about a baby who supposedly was consumed by rodents on the summit of Pike's Peak. The story was republished in papers from coast to coast. So many visitors believed the yarn and asked annoyed locals about it that practical jokers who worked for the Signal Service (the precursor of the US Weather Bureau) erected a fake gravestone to give them something to gape at.

The imitation grave lasted only until circa 1916, but it lives on in countless old tourist photos.

Hard Luck before and after Death

Pioneer Colorado was famous for its gold and silver mines, but one short-lived town made its fortune from coal: Crested Butte in Gunnison County. It is now a ghost town, and one reason may be the spectacular hard luck the community faced. On January 24, 1884, the Jokerville mine exploded with such force that mining cars flew out of the tunnel. Surface dwellers saw inky clouds rising from the shaft, and out of the smoke staggered twelve blackened men. "I know I crawled over several men that seemed very dead to me," remarked one.

Mine owners had installed a large ventilating fan in the shaft as a safety feature, believing that in case of an explosion, it would force out smoke and noxious fumes and allow in fresh air. It sounded great on paper, but under working conditions it trapped in smoke and kept out oxygen. Workers from other mines came to the rescue and after many hours extracted fifty-nine corpses. Many were found with handkerchiefs tied around their mouths, suggesting they had died from breathing poisonous gases rather than from the shock of the initial explosion or from burning.

Because it was wintertime and the ground was frozen solid, the multifarious dead were given shallow burials. Come springtime and the melting of snow, many caskets were exposed and had to be reburied with briskness.

Then in late February 1891, the snow that had fallen heavily on the mountain from which Crested Butte took its name came tumbling down on a camp near the coal mine. The mile-long avalanche killed a number of men, women, and children, including the family of Edward Clark, superintendent of the Bullion King mine.

Crested Butte became a ghost town but survives yet as a tourist attraction noted for its great skiing. It is also said to be haunted for some reason.

A Matter of Civic Pride

It may be just a legend, but it is said that when Georgetown was a new community the jealous citizens longed to have a cemetery just like all the other nearby towns. They got so impatient waiting for someone to die naturally that they jump-started their Boot Hill by hanging some miscreant.

Clifford's Plan

The town of Silver Plume—once a booming mining city, now more of a ghost town/tourist attraction—was incorporated in 1880. People in the area still talk about the creative demise of early citizen Clifford Griffin, born in Shropshire, England, then an immigrant to New York, then a Colorado pioneer. At Silver Plume, he and his brother discovered the Seven-Thirty Mine. Griffin was noted for his generosity; most mines started the morning shift at 6:30 a.m., but his opened at 7:30, hence its name. Every year he supplied each worker with a Dickensian Christmas goose, and every Fourth of July he paid their bar tabs. He also entertained the miners and their families with his violin.

Griffin got rich as the mine's manager but spent little of his wealth and was an object of curiosity for his solitary ways. He dwelt in a cabin on Columbia Mountain when he could easily have afforded a mansion. The story went that his fiancée had died on the eve of their wedding back in England—or had the tragedy occurred in New York? He declined to dignify the rumors with a response.

Griffin seemed to have two and only two hobbies: the first was spending his nights slowly, single-handedly digging a hole in the solid rock of Columbia Mountain. And after each night's labor Griffin would play sweet, sad melodies on his violin. As time went on, this hole became disturbingly the width and length of a man.

On the night of June 19, 1887, Griffin's miners heard violin music echoing from the mountain, followed by the discordant crash of a gunshot. They found thirty-nine-year-old Griffin stretched out in the grave he had dug. One wonders how long he had spent plotting his exit, which he had so gradually planned.

The suicide note in his office requested that he be buried in his self-made grave. The folks in Silver Plume did as he asked and erected a ten-foot granite monument atop his resting place. It is still there today, standing ostentatiously on the edge of a cliff.

12

WAY OUT WYOMING

Receding Hairlines

So how did it feel to be scalped by an Indian? Let's find out from a couple of men who knew from hard experience. One was pioneer Carroll B., who lived out his old age in San Francisco after an adventurous lifetime of Indian fighting and bear hunting. A reporter visiting him in 1888 noted that Carroll had long hair on the sides of his head but nowhere else: "If he lifts his long white hair from the side of his head he shows a great circular scar extending from above his right eye clear around the right side and back of his head almost to the left ear." Carroll told the tale:

> It was in '66, with the Sioux, and it was the worst brush I ever had with the Indians. They came upon a camp of nine of us and one of them pounced upon me, seized me by the hair, and cut right around my head where you see this scar. Then he gave a sharp wrench upward with his right arm and laid the whole skull bare. I cannot describe the pain it gave me, and I don't believe I could have endured any more without simply dying of it. There is no other torture man can be subjected to that will begin to compare with being scalped.
>
> It is a common belief that a man can't live after being scalped, but I've survived the experience a matter of twenty-two years, and I don't think I'm quite to the end of my journey yet, even if I am seventy years old. I knew another man up there, too, who didn't die under the scalping knife. The scalp was torn completely off from the whole top of his head, so that it had

to be constantly swathed in cotton and olive oil. He lived a year. That man knew what suffering means if ever a man did.

John T. of Hodgenville, Kentucky, also went prematurely bald the hard way. In May 1865, John was an army private stationed at Fort Leavenworth. As he and eleven other soldiers marched to Fort Connor (aka Fort Reno) in Wyoming, they were betrayed by a member of their own company and sent into the hands of Indians who ambushed the company and brained them with tomahawks and clubs. John fell unconscious after his skull was broken. He revived during his scalping. He must have been unusually adept at playing dead, as that is the only thing that saved him.

Finding all his companions dead, John crawled toward the fort and was rescued by a search party. For several months afterward, his survival was doubtful. John died on January 7, 1902, allegedly from the long-delayed effects of the scalping he'd received thirty-six years before.

A Literal and Figurative Ghost Town

How scary was the ghost that made its appearance in Latham, Sweetwater County, in January 1885? So scary that every living inhabitant abandoned the town, figuring that if the spirit wanted the place it could have it.

The ghost started off small by tapping on the windows and doors of postmaster Jasper O'Rourke's residence. These phenomena could easily be attributed to practical jokers, but then O'Rourke heard groans issuing from upstairs and under the floorboards. This too was somewhat explainable. But matters escalated as the specter got ambitious. The formerly invisible ghost manifested as a paper-white wraith that kept regular hours: it appeared between 11:00 p.m. and 4:00 a.m. After approaching O'Rourke's house from a distance, it would walk right through the walls without so much as saying "begging your pardon." It also went under or over the house when it wanted to.

O'Rourke had a second job as the section foreman for the Union Pacific railway. He had a dozen burly assistants from Ireland who swore they feared no revenants of the dead. But the ghost's nightly racket got to them too. On January 17, O'Rourke quit both of his jobs without giving advance notice, packed up his family, and made tracks for California. He sent the following telegram to his boss at the railroad, Eben Brown of Rawlins: "Here's my resignation. I am gone before you get this." As for the tough Irishmen, on January 18 they fled their huts en masse, preferring to work in the coal mines in Carbon.

The railroad was unable to find anyone willing to take O'Rourke's job; trainmen armed themselves when passing the town. On Saturday night, January 17, the Overland Express stopped at Latham. The train's brakeman, L. H. Foster, was unlocking the switch to sidetrack the engine when the ghost approached him. Foster dropped his lamp and fired four shots at the specter with his .45 caliber revolver. Engineer Pat Brown and fireman George Paige hurried to the scene and witnessed the ghost crossing the tracks as though it hadn't a care in the world. Some observers noticed that the redheaded Foster's hair took on a streak of gray after the incident.

Not long afterward, an "emigrant train"—probably loaded with people heading for California—pulled into Latham at night while waiting for engine no. 10 to arrive. The locomotive's engineer, Mr. Johnson, and his fireman fell asleep while waiting, only to be awakened by a deep voice inquiring, "What are you here for? Your train has gone." That woke the crew up fast, and the two men later swore the ghost had materialized between them in the cab. They started the train and took off so quickly they nearly collided with engine 10. Engineer Dowling aboard no. 10 saw the ghost exit the other train's cab and vanish across the prairie. After this, Latham had such a bad reputation among trainmen that engineers would perform necessary maintenance functions at the station before Latham rather than make a stop there.

Five citizens of Rawlins stayed overnight in abandoned Latham on January 20 to check out this ghost business for themselves. They heard the archetypical groans and wails but didn't see anything supernatural. Preacher and editor Mart C. Barrow described his experience in "the house" (presumably O'Rourke's) in facetious language obviously not intended to be taken seriously. Barrow claimed that after he had partaken of several drinks—to calm his nerves, ward away loneliness, and knock off the chill, of course—he had seen spooks aplenty and then some:

> Then the ghost himself showed up. He had a wagon-cover around him and his eyes glared most awfully. I put five .45-caliber balls through him as he stood in the door, but it never fazed him—I really thought he winked at me as I threw my empty revolver right through him. Then he took me by the collar and seizing a lantern gave me a run across the prairie for a mile or more—fact. When we got back to the house he disappeared—just winked out as it were—and I staggered in and finished what was left of that quart. You'd never believe me if I told you what took place after that. The whole house was filled with ghosts—big and little, male and female, men and women, birds, beasts and reptiles. Elephants waltzed with kangaroos and crocodiles shed tears at the sight. Monkeys played leapfrog and it made me dizzy to watch 'em, and huge snakes crawled about the room like [they

were] all possessed. And lizards and toads, he-goblins and she-goblins—the very air was filled with 'em!

The spirit presumably has lain low for some time or gone to wherever ghosts go when they retire, but no one can say for sure. Latham is abandoned to this very day.

Vintage Violence: Lynchings

George Francis Warden was better known as "Big-Nose" George Parrott. Judging from contemporary photographs, the nickname was not unjust. The desperado attained celebrity as a road agent in the region of Wyoming's Elk Mountains, but he went too far when he added wholesale attempted murder to his list of crimes. In 1878, his gang tried to derail a Union Pacific passenger train into a gorge 150 feet deep at Big Springs by pulling up the spikes in the tracks. Two deputy sheriffs were shot as they pursued the outlaws.

Parrott was arraigned for first-degree murder at Rawlins on September 12, 1880, and sentenced to hang. Parrott declined the advice of his attorney, stating that he did not want a trial and wished to pay for his misdeeds. It turned out to be a classic example of what can happen when we get what we wish for.

On December 15, Judge Peck sentenced Parrott to hang the following April 2. But around a week before the execution date, Parrott realized that maybe he didn't want to swing quite so badly after all. On March 23, 1881, Parrott slipped off his shackles and beat jailer Rankin with them. Mrs. Rankin sounded the alarm, and a masked mob broke into the jail. They carried Parrott to a telegraph pole, tied one end of a rope around his neck and the other end around the pole's crossbeam, and forced him to climb a ladder. Parrott cried, "I will jump off, boys, and break my neck."

Things didn't work out quite *that* well. Someone in the crowd kicked away the ladder before Parrott could jump to a relatively easy death. As he dangled by the neck, Parrott freed himself of his handcuffs and instinctively tried to climb the telegraph pole. He shouted, "For God's sake, someone shoot me! Don't let me choke to death!" Parrott finally slipped off the pole. Exhausted and weighed down by his leg irons, he strangled in midair. The friction of the noose abraded away his ears.

"Big-Nose" George's nose was so big the undertaker had difficulty closing the coffin lid. At last he gave up and nailed it shut, sending George to eternity with a squashed proboscis. This was by no means the final indignity visited upon Parrott. Dr. John Eugene Osborne exhumed the outlaw's body and removed the skin from his chest and thighs. He tanned these choice parts and converted them into a medical kit, a coin purse, and a snappy pair of two-toned shoes that the doctor wore as he made his rounds. He also removed the top of Parrott's skull to examine his evil brain. Dr. Osborne gave the skullcap to his assistant Lillian Heath, who knew exactly what to do with it. She put rocks in it and made it a doorstop.

Dr. Osborne became a congressman (1897–99), the third governor of Wyoming (1893–95), and assistant secretary of state (1913–16). Osborne allegedly wore his human footwear when he was inaugurated as governor. Lillian Heath won a measure of fame as the first woman doctor west of the Mississippi. Osborne donated his George shoes and a plaster death mask of the outlaw to the Rawlins National Bank; in a similar spirit of generosity, Heath gave the top of Parrott's skull to the Union Pacific Museum in Omaha.

The remainder of "Big-Nose" George turned up unexpectedly in 1950 when workmen in Rawlins excavated a whiskey barrel containing his skeleton, including his maimed skull. These bones are in the Carbon County Museum. If the ghost of George Parrott feels the urge to revisit his remains, he must be prepared to do a lot of traveling.

Among the inmates in the state penitentiary at Rawlings, grandmotherly Esther H. was called "the prisoners' friend." On September 29, 1912, someone outside the prison took advantage of Esther's kindness by criminally assaulting her in her home. It might have been Frank W.—at least he was arrested at Fort Steele on October 1 and temporarily placed in the prison. He was so unwise as to crack a joke about his guilt in the breakfast line the next morning. That was good enough for his fellow inmates, who seized him and hanged him from a cellhouse balcony rail, thus sparing a second mob surrounding the jail the trouble. The word around the jail was "the first man who squeals is the next man hung." That was sufficient to silence prisoners and guards who knew the identity of the lynchers. It remains a closely guarded secret.

A Room with a Boo

The first St. Mark's Episcopal Church was built in Cheyenne in 1868. A simple frame wooden church, it served until 1886, when the congregation decided they wanted a grander structure. In particular, they had their hearts set on an imposing bell tower. To this end, they hired a couple of Swedish master stonemasons to construct the new St. Mark's.

One day as the tower was under construction, one of the masons failed to show up at work. His fellow Swede explained that he was ill. The next day neither worker appeared. They never came back.

This presented a problem for the parishioners. The tower wasn't quite completed, and they could find no workmen with the skills to finish it as planned. New workers simply constructed a roof over the truncated tower, making a room near the top into a study for the rector.

However, it was by no means a *quiet* study. The room became notorious for the variety of uncanny sounds that echoed within it, including a voice and hammering. Considering that the tower walls were three to four feet thick and made of stone, it was unlikely the noises originated from outside. The voice was generally indecipherable, but one sentence stood out loud and clear: "There's a body in the wall." St. Mark's developed a reputation for being a haunted church in general and the tower's study room in particular.

In 1904, the study was sealed off. Decades ticked by; churchgoers were determined anew to have the tower's construction completed. In 1927—forty years after the project was begun—the church was finished, and St. Mark's Episcopal Church is still one of Cheyenne's architectural attractions. The tower is over eighty feet high, with eleven massive bells.

But there was the matter of that study. No one really wanted to use it. Someone had the idea of giving the study to the ghost so it would have a room of its very own. St. Mark's is one of the few structures in America that has a room specifically designated to be a ghost's living quarters (if that is the proper term).

It is said that many years after construction had begun on the tower, an elderly Swede in a Denver nursing home made a deathbed confession: he was one of the two tower stonemasons from 1886. One day, he said, his coworker had fallen and been instantly killed. But the Swedes had been in the country illegally, and the surviving workman thought it more expedient to wall up his friend's body than explain matters. He fled Cheyenne the next day, and the accident was never discovered. Interestingly, the church's rector in the 1970s had the walls x-rayed, and it was confirmed that bones of some sort were behind one. The wall was not opened, so it is unknown if the remains are human.

Rev. Rick Veit, current rector of St. Mark's, confirms that the study room in the tower is still there. It can be reached only by a narrow eighty-five-foot spiral staircase. The room measures twenty feet by twenty feet; is unheated; has a chandelier, a wooden floor, and walls painted a faint yellow; is unfurnished; and has three pointed Gothic windows facing east, south, and west. A bell room is above the study. The door is seldom opened, so the ghost, if there is one, has his privacy.

People still hear voices and odd noises in the church, including notes played on the organ. Reverend Veit has personally heard banging noises and creaking rafters but no voices. However, some parishioners claim to have heard them. Others declare they have seen Dr. George Rafter, who was the church's rector in the 1880s.

St. Mark's started Halloween tours in 2016. Not surprisingly, they are very popular.

13

OUTLANDISH OREGON

Bizarre Bequests

Capt. Henry Fraser T., a yachtsman who died in Portland on January 9, 1929, composed his will in nautical terms: "I . . . having struck a lee shore on my beam ends after sixty-six years of cruising on the sea of life, and it appearing that my cargo must be jettisoned, and desiring that it shall be possessed by those whom it is my will shall enjoy it, rather than by beachcombers, and being of sound mind and memory, and not acting under duress or undue influence of any person whomsoever, do now make, publish, and declare this my last will and testament in manner following. Once a sailor, etc. . . ."

In a Pickle

Twenty-three-year-old Aurilla S. passed to a better world on April 21, 1900, after she suffered a stroke while visiting a hospital. She was buried in Mount Hope Cemetery in Baker City. A little more than a year later, her father had her exhumed for reburial at Union. When he opened the coffin to have a final glimpse of Aurilla, he found, to his amazement, that her entire body had turned into what appeared to be "white marble." Accordingly, the 130-pound girl now weighed 200 pounds. The family decided to leave Aurilla right there in Baker City. Interestingly, the monument atop her grave also happens to be white marble.

Vintage Violence: Executions

Joseph Wade and B. H. Dalton shot James B. Morrow during a holdup gone wrong on November 14, 1901. Their total haul: twenty-five cents, or twelve and a half cents each if they split it. They were hanged at Portland on January 31, 1902. Just before the hangman put the noose around Wade's neck, the murderer said, "You may think I am happy, but I'm not."

On July 11, 1902, Alfred Lester Belding of Portland shot his wife, Maud; his mother-in-law, Mrs. L. McCroskey; and bartender Frank Woodward. Belding was tried and sentenced to death; his case was not helped when he boasted about his killing spree and said he wished to be hanged without delay. Multnomah County Sheriff William Storey expressed a plan to charge gawkers five dollars a head to see Belding's execution, which occurred on March 27, 1903. Storey wanted the money to provide for the upkeep of Belding's soon-to-be orphaned son. "I think it proper," said the sheriff, "that those receiving [tickets] who care to attend should contribute something to the support of the child whose father they have come to see hanged." Storey even offered to chip in the fee he would receive for hanging Belding. The prisoner himself thought charging admission was a neat idea.

The Pen Is Mightier

Llewellyn B. was a newspaper publisher who perhaps took his role as public crusader too seriously. He was convinced that a gang of political crooks was about to steal a local election. Perhaps Llewellyn was as bothered by the downward turn in his personal fortune as by perceived governmental chicanery; though a former millionaire, he had fallen on hard times. He had run for senator and been defeated. His newspaper, the *Medford Daily News*, was in financial ruin. His mansion and other property were on the verge of foreclosure.

Anyway, about that election: Llewellyn out-crooked the perceived crooks by stealing thousands of ballots from the county courthouse and stashing them in his mansion. He wasn't exactly subtle about it, either. He published an editorial warning that he would shoot anyone who came to his home and tried to serve him a warrant.

On the night of March 15, 1933, the grand jury indicted Llewellyn for burglary—what alternative did they have since he had confessed in print? The next day, Constable George P., who sometime earlier had seized newsprint from Llewellyn's office as part of a wage settlement for a former *Daily News* employee, went to the publisher's mansion with warrant in hand. If the officer had read that bellicose editorial, his heart probably wasn't in serving the writ. Llewellyn shot George dead as he approached the house.

Llewellyn turned himself in immediately and was arrested by some undoubtedly very nervous cops. He had to walk by George's body on the lawn to get to the police car.

"My husband had been trying to establish justice," cried the publisher's wife, adding, "He has been guilty of nothing except fighting the gang." Well, that, stealing ballots, and murdering an officer who had been acting in the line of duty.

Llewellyn defended his actions in a unique way: having an editorialist's gift with a pen, he created his own scoop by writing an explanation of his act and sending it to hundreds of newspapers across the nation via the United Press Syndicate. In his apologia, Llewellyn explained that he was sorry things had come to this but reminded readers that he *had* given fair warning: "Poor George. I am sorry for him, but under the circumstances I could not have acted differently and I would do the same thing again if anyone attempted to force his way into my home, as I have repeatedly warned them by letters and statements. [George] came to the door. Mrs. B. put the chain on the door and opened it. He tried to force it. She tried to hold him out. I warned him to keep away. . . . So I shot in defense of my home."

He complained again about those politicians, pointing out that fifteen of his acquaintances "have been arrested on charges of stealing ballots. Some are held without bond and without permission to have attorneys." As for the late Officer George P., "[He] is the man who took print from my property, the *Medford Daily News*. . . . It was a plot to cripple the *News*. . . . I've known George for a good many years. I supported him in the last election. But when he took the newsprint from my plant he was not acting in pursuance of his duty. He should have known better because we told him better."

This explanation was not satisfactory to the jury, which on May 21 found Llewellyn guilty of second-degree murder. It didn't help that his attorneys employed the wheeziest excuse of all, a plea of "transitory mania"—that is, temporary insanity. His wife was acquitted on charges of laying a trap for the officer.

Llewellyn was sentenced to a life term on August 14. I don't know the election results.

Murder in the Stars

Arthur Covell, age forty-seven, had cultivated both a sinister goatee and a reputation in the vicinity of Bandon and Marshfield—now Coos Bay—as an astrologer. He also had developed a hankering for murder. Problem was, he was permanently bedridden after breaking his back in a car wreck and was physically unable to carry out his plans. No problem: he figured out a plan for making *someone else* do the murdering for him. He simply hypnotized his sixteen-year-old nephew into doing the actual dirty work, or so the nephew claimed later when circumstances made it necessary to do some fast-talking.

The person Arthur wanted out of his way was his sister-in-law Mrs. Ebba Covell, who also happened to be his nephew's stepmother, on the grounds that she knew more about his past crimes and future plans than he thought safe. Arthur figured out from working a horoscope the most favorable time to murder Mrs. Covell. So it came to pass that on the morning of September 2, 1923, at the stars' recommendation, Arthur's nephew—thoroughly hypnotized!—sneaked up on Ebba as she worked in the kitchen, knocked her unconscious with a cloth soaked in ammonia, and strangled her.

Some sources claim that the nephew was mentally handicapped and therefore easily led. However, experts in hypnotism claim that no one can be mesmerized into performing an act that they would not be willing to do under ordinary circumstances. So it's hard to escape the suspicion that Arthur's nephew used his mystic uncle's "psychic influence" as a handy excuse—that is, *if* he were actually hypnotized at all. But who are we to say, really?

Unfortunately for stargazer Arthur, the heavens failed to alert him to trouble lurking on his own horizon. The ham-handed, amateurish crime was manifestly death by strangulation and promptly solved. The teenage nephew was arrested in short order. He confessed and blamed Uncle Arthur, whose niece confessed that she had helped move the body.

In Arthur's bedroom, police found a journal full of easily decoded gibberish and astrological signs. It was a damningly detailed plan of Ebba's murder, a veritable admission of guilt.

The jig was up, and Arthur Covell knew it. On October 9 he confessed, and how! Proudly acknowledging his role as puppet master, he also admitted his plans for a career in vicarious murder—*big* plans. Ebba's killing was just a dry run, an experiment. He thirsted to wipe out twelve prominent families in Coos County, twenty-seven people in all, their dates of extermination to be determined, of course, by signs from the heavenly bodies.

Criminologist L. S. May got his hands on several horoscopes Arthur had drawn. One proved Covell had his evil sights on wealthy dairyman E. J. Pressey. Covell intended to have his compliant nephew rob and murder Pressey, his wife, and their three children and then burn their house to disguise the crime—information that surely gave the Presseys a few sleepless nights. The crime was to be committed "when the family was under unfavorable planetary influence." The astrologer's hit list also included two merchants in Bandon. Furthermore, according to Mr. May, "The plans of Arthur Covell were so minutely detailed that they even called for the removal of windows and doors before the home of the victim was burned. The stolen articles were to be used in a home which the Covells intended to build. Even wills were to be written in evidence, turning the money over to the astrologer or his agents. One will was in the hands of the authorities when I left Marshfield, and it was so cleverly drawn up by him that it can hardly be detected as counterfeit."

In another case, Covell planned to murder a clothing dealer. According to a press account, "In accordance with his plot, the victim was to be found at the bottom of a stairway, indicating that he had fallen to an accidental death. In his pocket was to be found a will giving half of his property to Covell." No, that wouldn't have looked suspicious at all!

One might argue that had Covell been able to put his plan into action, he would have been the original Zodiac Killer. On October 13, the astrologer pled guilty to first-degree murder. He didn't even want to be represented by an attorney, which perhaps indicates a sense of guilt for what he had done. Or maybe the stars had informed him it was hopeless.

Arthur's trial commenced in November 1923. His physical infirmities required him to lie on a cot in the courtroom during the legal proceedings, but even so he did not win the jury's sympathy. They found him guilty and recommended that he be hanged like a painting, broken back or no.

In December, Arthur's nephew was sentenced to life in prison, where he worked as a cook. After serving nearly eleven years, he was pardoned in October 1934. He moved to northern California, then later to Texas, where he died in 2002.

Uncle Arthur did not meet such a happy ending. He kept his appointment with the hangman (though how could he refuse?) on May 22, 1925. Before his execution, petitions were circulated to commute his sentence, because a man who would influence his simpleminded nephew to commit a string of murders of entire unoffending families for profit is just the sort of guy you want to keep around.

Arthur Covell was cremated. His ashes are still stored at the Oregon State Hospital for relatives to receive, should any wish to claim him.

An Early Bigfoot Report?

I collect vintage newspaper accounts about Bigfoot just as other people collect baseball cards. One of the oldest in my collection is a surprisingly lengthy *New York Times* editorial dated April 26, 1871, which states that there have been nationwide reports of a hairy "wild man" and implies that just a few years after the Civil War stories about the cryptozoological creature were already well-known and widespread: "As most of our readers are probably aware, there is at present roaming over the United States and, for aught we know, making occasional excursions into British America [Canada, that is] and Mexico, a singular creature known as the 'Wild Man.' . . . At regular intervals of time he appears in different parts of the country, creating always great excitement in the neighborhood, and a vast deal of discussion in the local press."

Noting that this creature lived in the forest and allegedly had been sighted in Alabama, Oregon, and Tennessee, the editorial describes it in terms much like the canonical description of Sasquatch but with a notable lack of reference to oversize feet: "Accounts uniformly agree as to his appearance. He is preternaturally hirsute and ferocious, swift, and strong. . . . So far the received descriptions of him are unanimous." The creature had been seen in sizes varying from four to ten feet tall, which the ever-myopic *Times*—overlooking the possibility that there might have been more than one of them—found as absurd as his "seeming ubiquity" and the fact that the "wild man" was sometimes male and sometimes female.

The *Times* being the *Times*, the tenor of the editorial is to mock the very idea of an unknown apelike animal sneaking about in America and all the bumpkins who reported seeing it. A wild man captured in Michigan turned out to be a harmless lunatic, and an account from Soddy, Tennessee, was an obvious hoax, the supercilious editorialist wrote, and therefore all other reports may safely be discounted.

14

WEIRD WASHINGTON

Premature Burial

Charles Myers was separated from his wife. To teach her a lesson about abandoning a great catch like himself, he set fire to the hotel she managed in Asotin on March 16, 1893. Mrs. Myers escaped, but boarder Frank Sherry was killed.

Myers was hanged at Pomeroy on September 30, 1895, but may have survived his execution only to be buried alive. According to a contemporary news account, "It was stated by some who witnessed the execution that life was not entirely extinct when the body was cut down, and that if an electric battery had been applied immediately the man could have been resuscitated, for a faint pulse and respiration, it is said, were perceptible when the body was placed in the coffin."

On the other hand, Myers's story may have had a happy ending—for Myers, that is, not for the rest of society, which would have had an arsonist turned loose in its midst. On December 20, 1895, Henry Mather of Pomeroy declared that the murderer was alive and well, explaining that "after the hanging an old German who had taken charge of the body after it had been refused by relatives applied simple restorative remedies and resuscitated the apparently dead man." Henry said Myer was in hiding for fear that authorities would capture him, hang him again, and do a more professional job the second time. The district attorney doubted the story, stating emphatically that law enforcement officials had witnessed

Myers's burial in a potter's field. But perhaps Myers's friends had rescued him from the grave.

Mather wasn't the only person who claimed Myers had survived his hanging. According to a contemporary account, "two other men from Pomeroy have corroborated Mather's statement. These men positively assert that they personally saw Myers alive within the past week. They don't profess to be friends of Myers, but refuse to disclose where and under what circumstances or conditions they saw him."

Extraordinary Epitaph

Arthur J. Haine was the village atheist of Vancouver, and when he died in 1907 he wanted everyone to know his paltry claim to fame. His body was borne to his grave in a beer truck, and his gravestone in City Cemetery reads "Haine Hain't."

In a Pickle

Henry H. perished from kidney trouble in Ballard on the last day of May 1900. His family could not decide whether to bury him in Seattle or Michigan. Also, there was some question about the collection of his insurance money. In short, Henry was not finally laid to rest in Ballard's Mount Pleasant Cemetery for nearly a year after his passing.

Henry's remarkable state of preservation in that intervening year made an impression on his admiring contemporaries. His body had received only an average embalming, as it was thought at the time that he would be quickly buried. Despite the perfunctory treatment, Henry had not decomposed. Rather, his skin had turned slightly darker and hardened. "Another peculiar feature," said a clearly impressed newspaper account, "was that the body lost weight but did not fall away."

The Portrait That Aged

An unnamed Washington artist was noted in the closing days of the nineteenth century for a portrait of his wife. He had painted it in her youth, shortly after they were married. She died young, and for the rest of his life, on their wedding anniversary, the artist would "age" her likeness on the painting—that is, he would add a wrinkle here and a gray hair there to make her look the way he fancied she would have looked at that stage in her life, if she had survived. A person who saw the painting in 1899 described it: "Today the picture is that of an old woman, the hair turned gray, the face wrinkled and pale, but still beneath the marks of time, as made by the brush of the artist, can be seen the early beauty of the bride and the attractiveness of the young woman."

Sleep Slaying

Dr. Charles C. of Tacoma had a bad dream on the night of March 26, 1899, in which a dastardly stranger was about to stab his wife. The physician produced a revolver in his nightmare and fired twice at the villain. He awoke to find a smoking gun in his hand and his wife dead beside him.

That's the story he told the police. Many killers have claimed to have been asleep when they murdered, with varying degrees of success before investigators and juries, but in the grief-stricken doctor's case the authorities believed him. Dr. C. wasn't even arrested. The incident presumably broke him of his habit of keeping a loaded gun stashed under his pillow.

Good Heads for Business

In the years preceding the Civil War, Patkanim was chief of Washington's Snoqualmie (or Snoqualmoo) and Snohomish tribes at Puget Sound. At first he was adversarial toward the white settlers; the fact that his brother Quallawort had been hanged for conducting raids on settlers might have had something to do with it. However, he later changed his mind and became friendly.

During one uprising called the Puget Sound War of 1855–56, the US military offered a bounty of twenty dollars for each dead hostile Indian—that is, twenty dollars per head (literally). Patkanim saw this as a golden opportunity and went to war with the Klickitat tribe, from whom he secured a number of noggins. Patkanim decided this was too much work, and he sold the heads of his own Klickitat slaves, probably figuring the military wouldn't know the difference anyway. (Note that historians generally are reluctant to discuss the uncomfortable fact that Indians often enslaved rival tribes.)

The chief went to Olympia to collect his fee and returned to Puget Sound in high style, riding on the ship *Decatur* and preceded into the harbor by a fleet of twenty canoes. One pioneer described his fashionable togs, which sound like the mid-nineteenth-century equivalent of a pimp costume, including "congress gaiters, white kid gloves, white shirt with standing collar reaching halfway to his ears, and the whole finished off with a flaming red necktie."

The Territorial Auditor finally got suspicious and ended the practice of paying for heads, and thus ceased Patkanim's adventure in what today's cynical young social justice warriors might call decapit-alism.

Crashing the Party

Among the most memorable elements of the Charles Manson–directed Helter Skelter murders in Los Angeles were multiple corpses of the well-to-do found in their houses, overkilled in horrible ways with a variety of weapons. A case with eerie parallels occurred in Washington thirty-five years before, only the motive in the 1934 incident was much more down to earth than Manson's effort to trigger a race war: simple, unalloyed greed.

It all started with barking dogs. On March 31, 1934, two men in Erlands Point, a neighborhood seven miles northwest of Bremerton, noticed three French poodles were locked in a car that had been parked for three days in front of Frank Flieder's beach home at Ostrich Bay in Puget Sound. They peeped in a house window to see if everything was okay. After viewing overturned furniture everywhere and two bodies, they left the yard with understandable haste and called the sheriff.

When police broke open the door, they found something even worse than two bodies: four men and two women, dead two days at least. All were swollen and so badly beaten that at first officers could not tell if there had been one cause of death or several. The corpses' eyes and mouths were taped shut, their hands bound behind their backs with cord. Some had struggled so mightily before death that their bonds were loose. All of their heads were shockingly battered. The victims were:

1. Frank Flieder, age forty-five, a wealthy retired grocer. He was found lying facedown in the living room.
2. Mrs. Anna Flieder, age fifty-two, lying on her bed in a red dress.
3. Magnus Jordan, fifty, a retired navy officer, neighbor of the Flieders, and the house's caretaker. His body was in a chair in the sitting room.
4. Eugene Chenevert, thirty-eight, of Bremerton. He and his wife had been vaudeville performers under the stage names Bert and Peggy Vincent, and they had owned the car full of hot, hungry poodles. Chenevert had defensive wounds, indicating that he had fought his attacker. A former professional boxer, he must have given his assailant what for: Chenevert had been hit in the head twenty-two times with a hammer before he'd succumbed. He died in the living room gripping the leg of an overturned stool, as though trying to pull himself upright.
5. Mrs. Peggy Chenevert, thirty. She had died in the sitting room, her lower half on the floor and her upper half slumped on a daybed.
6. The fourth man was not identified at first but proved to be Fred Balsom, a bartender. He was crammed in a bedroom closet nearly hidden by clothes, his head propped up on pillows.

Weapons were left at the scene: a blackjack, a hammer, a meat cleaver, and a carving knife. One door bore a bullet hole, but the victims were so badly disfigured that it was not possible to tell at first if they had been shot. Later, autopsies confirmed that they had been. The killer had taken the gun with him.

The Flieders' ten-year-old daughter had been spared the carnage because she had been visiting her uncle for the past few days.

Even at this early stage of investigation, criminologists partially re-created the crime. The Flieders had been holding a social gathering when the party was crashed by an intruder—or, more likely, intruders. It was doubtful that a sole assailant could have controlled six people, even with a gun. The clear motive was burglary. The furniture was in a state of chaos. Broken liquor bottles, food, and plates were scattered on the kitchen floor; shelves had been overturned or torn off the walls; drawers' contents were dumped all around; and droplets of blood were sprinkled throughout the house. Most significantly, Mrs. Flieder's jewelry was missing, including diamond rings worth $2,100. All of the victims' pockets had been rifled. Police speculated that the burglars had tortured the Flieders and their guests to learn where $5,000 in bonds were hidden, which investigators found in Mrs. Flieder's safety deposit box.

As with most major murder cases, there were red herrings. A tailor reported that he recently had cleaned a bloody suit; the customer he named was taken in for questioning and released. A fifty-three-year-old Mt. Vernon man was arrested in Coeur d'Alene, Idaho, on the grounds that he had been in a fight and could not satisfactorily account for his whereabouts at the time of the murders. A marine saw three suspicious characters running out of the Flieder house one night after the murders had been discovered, but likely they were morbid curiosity seekers who just had to see the place for themselves. Victim Eugene Chenevert had killed a man named Hiram Roop in a 1929 fight in Stockton, California, and a relative of Roop's had sworn revenge. This promising clue, like the others, led nowhere.

The case was unsolved until mid-October 1935. Acting on a tip from the Seattle underworld, police came to believe Peggy Paulos, age twenty-seven, had something to do with the massacre. They arrested her, and two weeks later, on the advice of her lawyer, Peggy confessed that she had been an accomplice during the Flieder house murders. Back in March 1934 her acquaintance Leo Hall, a thirty-year-old Seattle dockworker and former athlete, had confided that he'd yearned to commit armed robbery. He'd had the Flieders in mind and wanted her to tag along. Foolishly she had agreed, thinking nothing worse would happen than a quick stickup and some easy money.

They hitchhiked from Bremerton to the Flieder beach cottage at Erlands Point. If Hall's intention was simply to rob the retired grocer and his wife, he made the fatal mistake of failing to ascertain beforehand whether they were alone. Once inside, Leo and his comely assistant were surprised to find a party underway and four occupants instead of two: Mrs. Flieder, Mrs. Chenevert, Mr. Jordan, and Mr. Balsom. Peggy helped Leo bind them. Then the crime in progress got even more complicated when two additional persons showed up: Mr. Flieder and Mr. Chenevert, who had gone to get beer. At some point the victims fought back, and Hall wildly stabbed, bludgeoned, and shot until the house resembled a butcher pen. Peggy fled the house in horror. Angered, Leo took a shot at her as she ran, but he missed.

Peggy also revealed how Leo had come to choose the Flieders as prey in the first place. Hall had overheard Mrs. Flieder mentioning her large income while patronizing a beer hall.

Leo Hall was arrested and questioned. He responded to police inquiries with all the considerable scorn and sarcasm he could muster, but he lost his smirk when a doctor told interviewers that he had treated Hall for a severe head wound the day after the murders.

Hall went on trial in December 1935. His codefendant, Peggy Paulos, the state's star witness, was acquitted, but Leo was convicted and sentenced to hang. On September 11, 1936, that's precisely what he did.

In Praise of Mrs. Smith's Superior Housecleaning Skills

On September 14, 1928, police in Oakland, California, pulled over sixty-three-year-old Mary Eleanor Smith and her thirty-two-year-old son, De Casto Earl Mayer. Smith and Mayer were driving a car that didn't belong to them. The interesting part was that the blue Chrysler 75 Roadster was registered to a missing person, naval officer Ens. James Eugene Bassett of Annapolis, whose recent disappearance in Washington as he drove across the country to join the United States Pacific Fleet was called "the Pacific Northwest's major mystery." The car contained Bassett's valuables, including his wallet, watch, and cuff links.

It was obvious that the elderly yet malevolent mother and her thuggish son, whom she called Earl, knew more about Bassett's disappearance than they were telling. Getting them to admit it was another matter. They stubbornly confessed nothing, and without a body the police couldn't prove a murder had occurred. Possession of a stolen car was the only charge that would stick. In short order, Mrs. Smith was serving an indeterminate sentence while Earl—who had a long rap sheet—was given a life sentence for being a habitual criminal.

Flash forward to May 4, 1938. Mary Eleanor Smith, now seventy-three, was about to be released from the state penitentiary in Walla Walla. She feared for the state of her soul and thought it wise to "get right with her Maker." For some weeks she had been writing incriminating letters about her past to a patrolman posing as a clergyman. She asked to see the warden, who granted her an interview.

She confirmed to this prison official what everyone had suspected all along: her son, Earl, had lured Bassett to his house in Bothell by feigning interest in purchasing his car but intending robbery and murder. "I was sitting on the couch, where I had a rod of iron hidden in a quilt in case of a struggle," said the dutiful mother. This wise precaution had proven unnecessary.

Earl had hit Bassett in the head with a hammer. Lest the reader form a low opinion of Earl, let it be noted that he was so sensitive to his mother's dainty feelings that he waited until she left the room before commencing the bludgeoning. "I heard the body fall and went back into the room. He was gurgling. I stepped out again and Earl gave him one more blow and it was all over. He never allowed his victims to suffer." (Note plural!)

Earl carried the young officer to the bathtub and dismembered his body with a meat saw and a butcher knife. After this physically taxing exercise, there was a touching moment of mother-son bonding. "The poor boy worked so hard," recalled Mrs. Smith. "To keep up his strength I made him an eggnog." Bits and pieces of Bassett spent the night in a galvanized iron tub in Earl's bedroom. Mrs. Smith admitted that she had been a trifle worried about this unseemly arrangement. What if Dr. Clark, from whom Earl was renting the house, should happen to drop by unexpectedly? *"That was one night! If Dr. Clark had called I would have had to admit there were indiscretions going on in the bedroom."* She would not wish her son to lose his social standing!

The next morning, mother and son removed evidence of these so-called "indiscretions" by putting most of Bassett, except his head and hands, in four sacks that were then buried in various locations in the forests north of Seattle. But they still had to do something with the leftover parts, so these most incriminating portions were tossed in a woodchuck hole.

While Mrs. Smith did not participate in the actual murder, or so she said, she couldn't refrain from boasting that she had cleaned the house so well that police searched the place in vain for forensic evidence. She also could not help taking motherly pride in watching officers ("those smart alecks") searching haplessly for clues: "They made perfect fools of themselves. No wonder Earl and I sat back in the old county jail in Seattle and laughed."

This confession was certainly a load off Mrs. Smith's mind, but on May 5 she unloaded more. She said Earl also had murdered Ole Larson of Anaconda, Montana, in 1921; Mrs. Ernest La Casse in Butte, Montana, in 1923; and David Randall, whom he had buried in an Idaho quarry. When asked what he thought about his mother's revelations, Earl sneered, "She's goofy!"

On May 7 Earl had a change of heart and admitted his mother was telling the truth. He added that he would plead guilty. His statement to the warden corroborated Mrs. Smith's. "I'm making this confession to take some pressure off my mother," Earl told the warden, so he must really have appreciated that frosty glass of eggnog. But what about the other three murders she had charged him with? Earl said he "would just as soon as not" admit those too: "I wouldn't give a damn if I pleaded guilty to the whole works."

And then more letters from Mrs. Smith were found suggesting that the mother-and-son team had committed nine murders at least. Needless to say, Mrs. Smith wasn't paroled after all. Prosecutor B. Gray Warner said, "There is no question but what she was the moving force and there is no reason for maudlin sentimentality here. I'll ask the jury to hang them both."

But neither maternal unit nor offspring ever faced the noose—at least not in a *professional* sense. On December 4, 1938, De Casto Earl Mayer hanged himself in his jail cell. He left a note addressed to his "Dearest Mother" saying he was tired of life. Prosecutor Warner thought his real motive was a desire to cheat the gallows.

Mrs. Smith was convicted of assisting in the murder of James Eugene Bassett, though his body had not been found. Her trial was attended by the missing man's mother, Mrs. Marion Bassett of Annapolis and Society Hill, SC. Noting that grief over his lost son had caused Mr. Bassett's premature demise, she stated that she did not wish for Mrs. Smith to receive the death penalty. "I'm an old woman, too," she told reporters. "I wouldn't want a cloud hanging over the rest of my life by asking that she hang. She will be just as well off in prison. Her death wouldn't bring back my boy." Of course, if Mrs. Smith spent life in prison that wouldn't bring her son back either, but no one pointed that out.

Perhaps because Mrs. Bassett urged clemency, Mrs. Smith was sentenced to life in prison—which turned out to be an amazingly long time. She died in 1966 at age one hundred. Hanging might well have been far more merciful. Evidently no fragment of James Eugene Bassett was ever found, nor any trace of Ole Larson, Mrs. Ernest La Casse, or David Randall. If Earl Mayer had killed them and hidden their bodies, he'd done the job very well, but then he may have inherited a certain efficiency from his mother.

An Ugly Incident in a Beautiful Location

On June 17, 1926, the body of twenty-two-year-old Sylvia Gaines was found on the shore of Green Lake in the Seattle neighborhood of the same name. She had been strangled, and the left side of her skull had been crushed with a rock. She seemed as low risk as a victim could get, being well-educated and a 1925 graduate of Smith College in Northampton, Massachusetts. Her family was respectable. In fact, her uncle was chairman of the board of county commissioners. Her father, Wallace Gaines, was a World War I veteran who suffered from what was then called shell shock, now known as post-traumatic stress disorder.

Sylvia had had an unsafe habit of going for evening strolls alone, but she'd always made sure to be home before it got dark. She had gone out for a walk on the evening of June 16 and hadn't returned, and then her body was found.

A married couple named Stokes stated that they had met Sylvia while she was walking, and she'd expressed concern about a roughly dressed man who seemed to be following her. The ruffian wasn't just a figment of her imagination; the Stokes saw him too.

A few details seemed trivial at the time but would reverberate later. Sylvia's parents had divorced when she was four years old, and she'd lived almost all her life with her mother in Lynnfield, Massachusetts. In September 1925, Sylvia had traveled to Seattle and moved in with her father. His second wife—who had shot herself the previous winter but survived—had been out of the house at the time, having spent the last four months in San Francisco. Wallace admitted that he and his daughter had had a minor quarrel about an automobile trip just before she'd gone for her stroll. At the inquest, Wallace admitted further that he had been drinking the night of Sylvia's murder.

The nebulous stalking creep might have seemed the obvious suspect, yet something about the victim's father bothered detectives. Perhaps they had heard rumors in the neighborhood; perhaps something about his demeanor was troubling. On June 26, the sheriff said, "We had our case when we had Wallace Gaines."

Wallace was outraged when he heard he was under suspicion, and the next day he *demanded* that he be put on trial so he could clear his name: "[The sheriff] says that I was the killer. Therefore, if there is a piece of evidence, I demand an immediate trial before a jury." The prosecutor refused on the grounds that he didn't have sufficient evidence to charge anyone—*yet*.

Wallace had told investigators previously that he and his second wife had "quarreled about Sylvia." The second Mrs. Gaines denied it, saying that her arguments with her husband had actually been over his prodigious alcohol consumption, which she said was the reason she had shot herself several months before.

Wallace's outraged wish to be arrested so he could clear everything up was granted on June 29. His defense team faced a major obstacle: Wallace's friend Louis Stern declared that Wallace had made a tearful confession on the night Sylvia had disappeared. According to Stern, Wallace had said, "You remember I always told you I'd be master in my own house; that if anyone tried to tell me what to do, or where and when to go or come, I'd kill them. That's just what happened."

The trial began in mid-August. The defense observed that the clothes Wallace had worn on the night in question were not bloodstained. The deputy coroner countered that Sylvia had been strangled before her battering, and if her heart hadn't been pumping there would have been little blood spattering. Over apoplectic defense objections, the prosecution introduced large crime scene photos showing Sylvia's body as it had been found. One strange feature: she had lain in one spot for a considerable time, then been dragged ten feet. The prosecution theorized that the murderer had left after killing her then returned to reposition the body and make the crime seem the work of a sex fiend.

An auto mechanic testified that he had noticed Wallace's car near the place where Sylvia's body had been found, at around the same time she had been killed. The defense attempted damage control by explaining that Wallace had been at a tire shop only two and a half miles from the death scene. But had the tire shop been open so late at night? If so, wouldn't it have been a simple matter to get confirming testimony from the clerk on duty that night?

Then the state's attorneys dropped the other shoe. They declared that if Wallace were acquitted of murder, he would be arrested for committing incest with his daughter. How exactly they proved this charge was not reported by the newspapers, but apparently it was substantiated in queasy detail. It could be argued, of course, that while this revelation explained Wallace's motive, it also prejudiced jurors so much against him that his conviction was a foregone conclusion.

Louis Stern told his story about the incriminating confession the father had made on the night Sylvia had vanished. He was followed by defense witness John Mullane, who said Louis had told him the same story. Mullane also admitted that he'd seen a cut on Wallace's left thumb the morning after the murder.

One of Wallace's attorneys thundered that the defense would *prove* Sylvia's killer had returned to the scene of the crime that night—and he was *not* Wallace Gaines! But, the lawyer added most anticlimactically, the "defense would not be able to name or identify this man."

As the case wound down, it featured a bizarre sidenote: one of the state's investigators, Robert Glanville, was found dead in Seattle in a sealed room full of gas on August 17. A wishy-washy suicide note read, "Goodbye. I am kind of disappointed." But the coroner thought that the handwriting looked forged and ordered an investigation. The next day he decided the cause of death had been self-asphyxiation after all.

Wallace's case went to the jury on August 18. The deputy prosecutor said in his summation, "The purpose of introducing evidence of unnatural relations between the defendant and his daughter was not to prejudice the jury, but to show motive." Prejudicial or not, after only four hours' deliberation the jury found Wallace guilty and recommended the death penalty.

On August 31, 1928, Wallace mounted the scaffold at the Walla Walla state penitentiary, protesting his innocence to the very last. The matter is still debated in Seattle.

The Unanswered Question

Dr. Paul M. of Calhoun, Kentucky, seemed to have it made. A 1908 graduate of the University of Louisville medical school, in 1920 he moved to Sequim, Washington, with his wife of twenty-five years. There he established a private sanitarium, Sequim Prairie Hospital.

On July 4, 1926, his wife came down with a liver ailment. She checked in to her husband's hospital, where he instructed a nurse to give Mrs. M. pills he provided. Mrs. M. underwent an operation on July 10 and died on July 20 of what was deemed "abscess of the liver." Just before the patient died, a Dr. J. became suspicious of the pills, but it was too late to help her. He told authorities that he thought there was more to the death than met the eye. They in turn theorized that when Mrs. M. had gotten sick, her husband had seen an opportunity to rid himself of her. The body was exhumed by the eerie glow of car headlights on the night of August 31. A Seattle pathologist found traces of poison in Mrs. M.'s stomach; he removed a few grains and injected them into a guinea pig, which died forty-eight minutes later.

As the doctor visited a brother in Nashville on September 4, he was arrested due to these and other fishy circumstances: when the nurse had asked the doctor to help hold down his dying wife after she'd begun convulsing, he'd refused on the grounds that he just couldn't bear to watch. But it appeared that there was another woman whom he was not at all averse to holding. The doctor and his wife were known to have quarreled over his perhaps too-close friendship with Mrs. William K.

Just after Mrs. M.'s funeral, the doctor and Mrs. K. had made a joint disappearance; their timing couldn't have been tackier. Certainly the missing woman's incensed husband had thought they were up to something, because he vowed that if they were found he would file charges against the doctor under the Mann Act, a law that made it a felony to transport "any woman or girl for the purpose of prostitution or debauchery, or for any other immoral purpose." Mr. K. wasn't fooling around, even if his wife was.

While in Tennessee, Dr. M. had responded that it was all a plot by Mr. K. to ruin his reputation and beggar him: "The enmity grew from [his] objections to frequent professional visits made by [Mrs. K.], who was being treated for cancer." He didn't explain why he and his patient had both vanished for several days and at the same time. He added that he didn't believe his colleague Dr. J. and the nurse had made any such charges against him—it was all a tall tale by the jealous Mr. K. (Later, Dr. J. and the nurse would repeat the very same stories under oath.)

More to the point, Dr. M. asked why no action had been taken if Dr. J. had suspected poisoning *before* the patient had died. Dr. M. added that he had remained in Sequim two weeks after her death before he'd gone east to visit relatives, and the authorities had been free to question or arrest him at any time.

Once extradited to Washington, Dr. M. did not stay in jail long. A dozen Port Angeles and Sequim residents secured his $30,000 bail, and he was freed. This suggests that the community held him in high esteem.

The trial began on November 15. At first things did not look good for the doctor. A pharmacy clerk testified that he had seen Dr. M. filling a capsule a few days before his wife had died. His so-called rival at the hospital, Dr. J., testified that his colleague had expressed grave doubts that his wife would recover and even predicted that she would die nine days after the operation. She had died on the tenth day, so his morbid diagnosis had been only slightly off.

James B., a druggist, said under oath that in June 1926 Dr. M. had asked him how much of a certain poison it would take "to get rid of an animal around the house." Dr. B. had noticed a bottle of this poison on Dr. M.'s shelf.

The nurse assigned to give Mrs. M. her medicine reported two statements made by Dr. M. that sounded heartless even if one gave them an innocuous interpretation. The day after the operation, he had asked his wife if her pain was better. When she'd said yes, he'd replied, "Don't worry. It will be back presently." After she had died, the doctor had told the nurse, "I told you she would die in convulsions. They can't put anything over on me. In Kentucky they always die in convulsions after an operation like this."

Then, on November 17, a setback for the prosecution: the judge ruled that "immoral conduct of the husband is an immaterial matter unless connected in some way with the commission of the crime." The jurors did not hear about the alleged sleazy behavior between Dr. M. and Mrs. K., thereby depriving the state of the chance to relate a possible motive. (At the time Mr. K. was divorcing his wife, so he was convinced the charges of adultery were true.)

On November 19, the jury acquitted Dr. M. after slightly more than four hours' deliberation. But his troubles were not entirely behind him. Mr. K. evidently gave up the idea of pressing Mann Act charges against him but did the next best thing. On December 30, he slapped Dr. M. with a $25,000 suit for alienating his wife's affections.

It is a fact that poison was found in Mrs. M.'s body. The big question remains unanswered: if her husband didn't put it there, who did?

George's Jig

George M.'s friends were lounging around in Riordon's Saloon in Vancouver on that lazy October 6, 1904, when, to their surprise, George burst out of the back room, a winning grin on his face and dancing, dancing, dancing! His high-stepping became noticeably less energetic as time passed. Within ten minutes he was lying on the floor and beyond medical aid. His friends learned that just before his public display, he had swallowed an ounce of carbolic acid. Perhaps they should have been tipped off when he remarked, "Well, boys, here's for the long sleep" just before entering the saloon's back room.

An Ounce of Prevention Is Worth a Body in a Tree

Desperado Calvin Pierce shot George Curtis in April 1884 in Grand Ronde, Oregon. The murder was unprovoked, yet a jury acquitted him. Locals who happened not to be on the jury were so peeved that they gave Pierce the customary twenty-four hours to leave the vicinity.

Pierce fled to the Palouse River in Washington Territory, where he became a miner at the Hoodoo Diggings camp. He lost none of his bad habits despite his previous close shave with the law: early in 1885, he tried to pick a fight with a young miner named W. H. Newcome, who declined the honor. As Newcome returned to work on his claim, Pierce sneaked up behind him and cleft his head in twain with a pickax.

Pierce escaped, but a company of vigilante miners tracked him, tried him, found him guilty, and sentenced him to immediate death by lynching. He was left swinging in one of Washington's beautiful, majestic trees on February 18, 1885. The jurors back in Oregon were left to contemplate how their unaccountable leniency resulted in two more deaths.

Mr. Tracy Goes Camping

At first, Harry Tracy—whose real name, it appears, was Harry Severns—was the average Western bad man. In 1897, he murdered cattleman Valentine Hoge and a boy named William Strong in Colorado. Then one day Tracy decided to go for broke and cemented his reputation as one of the West's last true old-school outlaws. That life-changing event occurred on June 9, 1902, when Tracy and his brother-in-law David Merrill escaped from the Oregon State Penitentiary in Salem. On the way out, they killed three guards and wounded a fellow convict named Frank Ingraham (some accounts say Ingram), who tried to foil their plan. Ingraham's leg had to be amputated.

There was no turning back, so the escapees figured they might as well get into as much trouble as possible. The day after they escaped, they held up a man near Salem, taking his food, clothing, and horses. They improved on this feat on the way to Portland by robbing two members of the posse following them of their horse and buggy.

On June 11, they ambushed a posse near Gervais and continued their flight.

On June 12, they were surrounded by a large segment of the Oregon militia numbering 250 men. It seemed impossible for Tracy and Merrill to escape—yet they did, sneaking by the posse at night. Two days later they stole horses near Oregon City and brazenly rode through Portland's suburbs.

On June 15, they forced boatmen to row them across the Columbia. They landed five miles above Vancouver, Washington, and disappeared into the forest. By crossing the state line, they made their depredations a federal matter rather than merely Oregon's concern.

On June 17, the desperados exchanged fire with the posse at Salmon Creek and escaped, then stole fresh horses at Ridgeford.

By this point, the flight of Tracy and Merrill had become a topic of national interest. Few things intrigue the public more than an outlaw on the run. People wonder, will he be caught? If so, when? Most importantly, am I going to be so unlucky as to run into him? The nation's newspapers kept a daily record of the escapees' antisocial antics, somewhat reminiscent of a sports page following the ups and downs of a football team.

The outlaws stole clothes and money from a rancher in La Center on June 22, swiped a hearty breakfast in Kelso on June 25, abstracted two more horses on June 26, and escaped another large posse in Chehalis on June 29.

The duo was spotted walking the Northern Pacific railroad tracks in Tenino on July 1. Around this time Merrill disappeared, and all sightings of Tracy thereafter were solo appearances.

On July 2, Tracy held up six men at a restaurant near South Bay. He forced them to give him a ride to Seattle in an oyster boat. During the voyage he confided that he had murdered his partner, Merrill. The boat's captain Clark told reporters, "All day he displayed the most daring recklessness regarding the taking of human life, and all day he exercised the most exacting vigilance to prevent us from getting the drop on him in any manner."

Tracy shed more blood in Bothell on July 3, killing Deputy Sheriff Charles Raymond of Snohomish County and Deputy Sheriff Jack Williams of Seattle, and wounded two reporters. Later that day, Tracy killed policeman E. E. Dreese (Breeze or Bresse in some accounts) in Fremont and game warden Neil Rawley. The outlaw ended this busy day by camping overnight in a cemetery.

If Harry Tracy showed a talent for anything, it was for getting out of seemingly inescapable traps. On July 4, the roads within a twenty-mile radius of Seattle were patrolled by armed guards—and hundreds of armed citizens, each of whom craved the glory of being the person who shot Tracy—but the outlaw vanished like a ghost. He turned up near Ballard, where he swiped a horse and buggy. Before stealing the items, he revealed his identity to the occupants by defiantly shouting, "Harry Tracy!" The warning was sufficient; the homeowners meekly stayed inside. After this, Tracy forced a Madison Point boy to row him to Meadow Point. He spent the night in the home of a farmer named Fisher, reading news accounts of his feats and commanding Mrs. Fisher to cook several days' worth of food. He left after resting for several hours.

On July 5, he invaded the home of a rancher named Johnson near Madison Point. He told the family that his original intention was to kill everyone in the house and hide out for a few days. He added, "But after seeing your pretty little girl, I will kill no one if you all mind me. I will be here all day." Again he avidly read the latest newspaper accounts of his exploits, complaining that it had been "necessary" to kill Raymond and Williams because a witness had tipped them off to his whereabouts.

After enjoying a meal and a good read, Tracy ordered the Johnsons to give him food to go and a new set of clothes. He tied up the family and ordered their hired hand, John Anderson, to row him across the sound. Mrs. Johnson got free two hours later and informed the authorities, who set off in hot pursuit. One matter deeply concerned the lawmen and the Johnsons: what did Tracy intend to do with the abducted laborer Anderson? The press surmised that the fugitive would kill Anderson the moment he was no longer of any use.

Thanks to Mrs. Johnson, the posses had at least some idea where Harry Tracy might be headed, and they guarded all avenues of escape. They patrolled roads, forests, and waterways. Yet he escaped with ease, as though he had merely walked through a park.

On July 7, Tracy's abandoned boat was found at the head of Miller's Bay. There was little hope that Anderson would be found alive; Tracy already had wounded six and killed eight, if he told the truth about killing his jailbreak partner, Merrill. But two sets of tracks led from the ditched boat into the forest, suggesting that the hostage was alive. On this day Tracy came within a few hours of being captured, but his phenomenal luck held. Police received word from a teenage boy named Gerald (some accounts say Grennell) that Tracy was hiding at the Geralds' home near Renton. The boy even had two watches stolen from the Johnson family that Tracy had ordered him to sell. Fifty armed men with bloodhounds hustled to Mrs. Gerald's house. Imagine their disappointment when she told them that Tracy had indeed been there but fled ten minutes before they had arrived! On the positive side, they found the Johnsons' hired man, Anderson, alive, tied to a tree in the backyard and with a great story to tell his future grandchildren.

Still, Tracy had only ten minutes' lead time on the posse. A thousand men and their dogs pursued him through Washington's forests. End result: nothing but footprints, cursing men, and exhausted bloodhounds. The rescued Anderson revealed that Tracy had accomplices who helped him during his flight, which may explain how he performed so many seemingly miraculous escapes. While on his unwilling journey, Anderson saw Tracy meet four friends at the Black River Bridge, including a fellow Tracy greeted as Fred. Another of Tracy's tricks to avoid capture was sprinkling cayenne pepper in his tracks to baffle bloodhounds.

Tracy was bound to run out of supplies, and when he did he would have to perform another home invasion to restock. True to form, he entered the house of E. M. Johnson two miles from Kent on July 9. Tracy ordered Mr. Johnson to go to Tacoma and buy him a new revolver, ammunition, and provisions, promising that if Johnson failed to do so or informed the law he would murder the rest of the family. Johnson did as commanded. When Tracy fled and it was safe to talk about it, Johnson said his visitor was suffering from extreme exhaustion.

On July 10, Tracy and a posse exchanged fire near Covington; ditto at Sluice Creek on July 11. He escaped both times but was wounded during the Sluice Creek incident. It was thought that his capture was now certain. He was surrounded in the countryside between Covington, Franklin, and Ravensdale. All roads, trains, and farmhouses were being watched, so how could he possibly escape the dragnet? And yet Tracy would elude his pursuers for nearly another month.

On July 12, he passed the house of Frank Pautoto near Black Diamond. The escapee said nothing to the rancher, but Pautoto was so terrified by the sighting that he spent the night at a neighbor's house.

National interest in Harry Tracy reached a fever pitch. The Apache chief Geronimo expressed a desire to hunt him down. The chief was something of an expert at hiding from pursuers, his own capture having cost the US government $5 million.

Another who was adept in the art of hiding from lawmen, Frank James—Jesse's brother, now respectably retired from outlawry—told a reporter that the only way to catch Tracy would be to trap him in a crowd. James predicted, "I should say that Tracy will never be captured alive. He will fight to the last ditch and be killed rather than be taken."

On July 28, an imprudent man named William Nixon told a Seattle music hall actress that he was the infamous outlaw Tracy. Most likely he was trying to impress her, and he ended his confidences by threatening to murder her if she tattled. But she did tell, and the next thing the Tracy impersonator knew, he was being pounded like plaster by a policeman and the theater's owner, Joe Williams, who happened to be the brother of Jack Williams, the lawman shot by the genuine Tracy. Nixon was considered very fortunate to have been merely beaten instead of shot or lynched.

On July 14, a woman named Mrs. Mary Wagner (Wagoner in some accounts) and her twelve-year-old son were picking berries in Chehalis, Washington, when they found the badly decomposed body of a man who had been shot in the back and neck and thrown over a log. It wasn't too ripe to be recognizable, however, and the law found that Harry Tracy had told the truth when he'd said he'd killed his partner, David Merrill. Mrs. Wagner personally hauled her smelly prize to the Oregon State Penitentiary and demanded the $1,500 "dead or alive" reward the state had promised. The warden made a counter offer of only $300; insulted, Mrs. Wagoner said she wanted the full reward. The state of Oregon ended up paying her nothing, but she was wealthier in the sense that she had a really good story to tell about transporting a dead outlaw over a hundred miles. This turn of events dampened the enthusiasm of the various posses chasing Tracy, who realized that they might get no reward for killing or capturing him—other than the inner satisfaction one gets from doing the right thing, of course. This, plus the fact that the lawmen frankly admitted they had no idea of Tracy's present location, made them seem on the verge of giving up.

Perhaps it was due to sheer frustration, but on July 19, after forty days of fruitless searching at a cost of $10,000 to the Washington counties of Clark, Cowlitz, Lewis, Thurston, Pierce, Kitsap, Snohomish, and King, the manhunt for Harry Tracy was called off. Also, as one news account noted, "The fact that Oregon declines to pay . . . the reward for Merrill's body has done much toward the flat drop of the Tracy hunt." On the other hand, former outlaw Frank James opined that the police falsely told the press they were giving up the search, knowing that Tracy was addicted to reading newspaper reports about himself and might let his guard down.

Tracy turned up again on July 23 at a logging camp near Kanaskat, fresh as a daisy, in good spirits, seemingly unwounded, and well stocked with a rifle, two revolvers, plenty of ammo, and a spiffy new derby. In early August, he was reportedly heading for Idaho and intended to go from there to the veritable outlaws' paradise known as the "Hole in the Wall" territory in Wyoming, a favorite hideout of Butch Cassidy and his gang. Said one account, "When there, he declares, he will be a thief among thieves and thinks he will be safe."

Tracy's luck had to end sometime. On August 3, he sauntered onto the L. B. Eddy ranch near Davenport. Just as the police and press had speculated, he almost made it to the Idaho border. Tracy's established method of getting supplies, as already noted, was sending some terrorized person on errands under threat of death; this time it backfired. After making eighteen-year-old G. E. Goldfinch his involuntary servant for two days, Tracy told Goldfinch he could leave but promised to kill him if he revealed his whereabouts. Goldfinch was not cowed, and once in town he told people that Tracy was hiding at the Eddy ranch.

On August 6, five men from Creston who had heard about Tracy's presence came to the ranch armed to the teeth. The outlaw saw them approaching, grabbed a rifle, and hid behind a haystack. After exchanging shots, Tracy chose to make a run for a boulder. Just as he got to it, he was shot twice in the leg. He crawled into a wheat field and hid there until sundown. He was too weak from loss of blood to escape, and, knowing capture was inevitable, he fulfilled Frank James's prediction by shooting himself in the head. The posse waited until the morning light confirmed his death. He died wearing, of all things, a bicycle cap. (Tracy's body was photographed where it lay in the wheat field. The photo became a popular collector's item and can easily be found on a number of websites.) A newspaper account noted, "After baffling the officers of two states, after a wonderful flight of nearly 400 miles across Oregon and Washington, Tracy was hunted down by four citizens . . . and a sole Deputy Sheriff."

The inquest on Harry Tracy's body was held on August 7. Then came two inevitable and unpleasant circumstances: an argument over who was entitled to the reward, and a morbidly curious throng's rush for relics of the dead outlaw. A crowd of hundreds followed the wagon containing Tracy's body up the streets of Davenport. Members of the posse kept Tracy's unfired bullets as souvenirs, but other citizens rushed the morgue, and—well, here's how a reporter described the ensuing unflattering commentary on human nature:

> Several persons were allowed to see the body, and then trouble began. Everyone wanted a relic, and in a short time nothing was left but the body. Someone even picked up the bloodstained handkerchief which had been used by the outlaw to keep from bleeding to death. Before he could carry the awful relic away he had to do it up in paper, as it was too wet to place in his pocket. Someone got the strap which had been pulled around his leg to keep him from bleeding to death. That, too, was soaked with blood which ran from the upper wound. Many locks of the outlaw's hair were carried away, and in some places his head had been made bald. His trousers were cut into strips, and before they were divided they were cut into smaller pieces.

No word as to who got Tracy's nifty bicycle cap. Perhaps some of these ghoulish keepsakes exist yet in trunks and attics. But this was not the end of the indignities performed on the desperado's body. Once it arrived at the Oregon State Penitentiary for burial on August 9, the coffin was placed in the prison chapel so the convicts could pay their respects. After which, officials buried him in the prison cemetery—but not before pouring vitriol over the corpse's face to make his remains less tempting to body snatchers who might wish to dig up Harry and put him on exhibit. The jail superintendent kept Tracy's rifle.

A few more droll anecdotes, and then we shall close the curtain. A highwayman who held up farmers near Spokane after August 6 claimed to be Harry Tracy; evidently this genius hadn't read the newspapers.

Tracy's hold on the public imagination was still strong as late as 1912, when someone produced a play called *Tracy the Bandit*. The melodrama glossed over the fact that Tracy was a murderer several times over. One review described the characterization of the outlaw, which is typical of the human urge to sentimentalize killers: "Bandit Tracy is rather a clean sort of a chap, according to the conception of the dramatist, going about doing more good than harm. It is his desire to be a protector rather than a disturber that gets him into trouble." Dave Merrill appears as a character in the play. In real life, of course, Tracy shot him in the back while on the run.

Remember that when breaking out of jail in Oregon, Tracy and Merrill wounded a fellow prisoner named Frank Ingraham. He had been serving a life sentence for murdering his brother, but the governor gave him a pardon as a reward for his bravery in attempting to stop Tracy and Merrill. Ingraham moved to San Jose, California, where he died in 1916. His will requested that his amputated leg be exhumed from the prison cemetery back in Oregon and reunited with the rest of his body before burial.

BIBLIOGRAPHY

Terrifying Texas

Your Friendly Neighborhood Ax Murder Cult

Daily Picayune (New Orleans). "Another Arrest Made in the Bernarbet Case." April 6, 1912, 1+.
———. "Ax Man Causes Terror." April 19, 1912, 3.
———. "Axman Killed Five." April 13, 1912, 1.
———. "Ax-Murder Trial at October Term." August 19, 1912, 12.
———. "Ax-Wilder Puts Family to Death." November 23, 1912, 14.
———. "Bernarbet Girl Found to Be Sane." October 22, 1912, 16.
———. "Jury to Take Up Bernarbet Case." October 8, 1912, 15.
———. "Just Escaped Noose." April 19, 1912, 16.
———. "Life Term Given Bernarbet Woman." October 26, 1912, 1+.
———. "Lunacy Board May Examine Her Mind." October 17, 1912, 14.
———. "Negress Is Indicted for Murdering Family." April 5, 1912, 1+.
———. "Negro Charm Seller Held . . ." April 4, 1912, 1+.
———. "Official Stretch Dragnet and Get Woman." April 7, 1912, 1+.
———. "Officials Think That Woman Had Accomplice." April 3, 1912, 1+.
———. "Says She Slew Twenty Blacks." April 2, 1912, 1.
———. "Wielder of Deadly Ax Not Arraigned." April 9, 1912, 1+.
Louisville Courier-Journal. "'Axwoman' Confessed to Killing Nineteen." October 25, 1912, 7.
———. "Confessed Murderer of Seventeen Is Indicted." April 5, 1912, 2.
———. "Family of Six Butchered." November 29, 1911, 2.
———. "Five Members of Family Killed While They Slept." April 13, 1912, 8.
———. "Heads of Six Negros Crushed with Ax." March 28, 1912, 8.
———. "'Negro Ax-Woman' Is Sentenced to Prison." October 26, 1912, 2.
———. "Negro Family of 5 Murdered in Louisiana." January 27, 1912, 2.
———. "Negro Girl as Human Butcher." April 3, 1912, 1.
———. "Police Capture 'Voodoo Doctor.'" April 4, 1912, 4.
———. "Sanity Court for Woman Accused . . ." October 19, 1912, 2.

———. "Seventh of Series of Similar Crimes Occurs." February 20, 1912, 2.
———. "Sparks from the Wires." January 23, 1912, 13.
———. "Three Other Families Marked for Sacrifice." April 9, 1912, 4.
———. "Trial of Negro 'Ax Woman' to Begin To-Morrow." October 23, 1912, 7.

Texas Pastimes

"John Chapman v. the State." *Texas Criminal Reports* 43 (1903): 328–40.
Louisville Courier-Journal. "Beaten to Death in a Fight with Cowboys." May 19, 1903, 3.
———. "Ice Man Sentenced to 50 Years . . ." April 6, 1936, 1+.
———. "Kentucky News in Brief." March 6, 1901, 5.
———. "Kidnappers Get 'Wrong Man' . . ." May 26, 1934, 1+.
———. "Man's Murder Laid to His Son, Daughter." December 29, 1934, 7.
———. "Removed to Fort Worth." December 5, 1900, 4.
———. "Roasted While Men Stood by and Jeered." December 4, 1900, 1.
———. "Slain Because He Wore a Silk Hat." May 19, 1903, 6.
———. "Texan Cooked Family of Four." March 15, 1936, I, 1.
———. "Third Confesses Burying Man Alive . . ." November 19, 1935, 1+.
———. "With Dynamite He Blew Himself Up . . ." April 10, 1896, 5.
New York Times. "Tied to a Stake in the Woods." February 16, 1884, 2.
Sedalia [MO] *Democrat*. "Convicted of Burning a Constable to Death." December 6, 1901, 3.

Four on a Limb

Franscell, Ron. *The Crime Buff's Guide to Outlaw Texas*. Guilford, CT: Globe Pequot Press, 2011.

Advance Notice

Louisville Courier-Journal. "Southern News." July 10, 1879, 2.

Work Shirkers

Louisville Courier-Journal. "Convict Bored by Work . . ." May 14, 1937, III, 10.
———. "Convict Forcing Snake to Bite . . ." June 12, 1937, II, 12.

Leave 'em Laughing

Louisville Courier-Journal. "He Died Laughing." April 18, 1886, 7.

Sinkhole and Stinkhole

Franscell, Ron. *The Crime Buff's Guide to Outlaw Texas*. Guilford, CT: Globe Pequot Press, 2011.
Robertson, Katelynn. "The Sinister Origin of Dead Man's Hole." *Texas Hill Country*. July 19, 2016. http://texashillcountry.com/dead-mans-hole-burnet-county/.

A Hotel Fit for Ghosts

Givens, Murphy. "The Alta Vista Hotel." *Corpus Christi Libraries*. Last modified June 2008. http://cclibraries.com/archives/radioaltavista.htm.
Louisville Courier-Journal. "The Relic of a Boom." September 11, 1897, 9.

The Joy of Sects, or: No Sects with Men

Lamanna, Mary Ann, and Jayme A. Sokolow. "Belton Woman's Commonwealth." *Texas State Historical Association*. Last modified August 9, 2017. https://tshaonline.org/handbook/online/articles/vib01.

Louisville Courier-Journal. "A Sect of Women Only." July 23, 1899, III, 4.

———. "A Queer Sect of Women." September 28, 1895, 11.

An Incompatible Traveling Companion

Louisville Courier-Journal. "Admits Killing Widow." August 19, 1934, I, 4.

———. "Girl's Nude Body Is Found in Texas." November 8, 1933, 1.

———. "Man Describes Killing Widow." August 20, 1934, 3.

———. "Wilson Found Guilty of Desert Slaying." December 14, 1934, I, 10.

Kumbaya

Franscell, Ron. *The Crime Buff's Guide to Outlaw Texas*. Guilford, CT: Globe Pequot Press, 2011.

Whitington, Mitchel. *Angels of Oakwood: Jefferson's Historic Cemetery*. Jefferson, TX: 23 House Publishing, 2006.

Homegrown Massacres

Louisville Courier-Journal. "Crazed Man Accused of Murdering 9 Kin." December 24, 1926, 1+.

———. "Hassell Killed 4, Is Discovery." February 2, 1927, 16.

———. "Killer of 9 Boasts He Has Slain 4 More." December 28, 1926, 1.

———. "Mother Dies, but Fails to Kill Her Son, 7." March 19, 1938, I, 7.

———. "Mother Gets 495 Years for Killing Children." April 7, 1938, I, 14.

———. "Mother Kills 6 Children as They Sleep." March 18, 1938, I, 11.

———. "Murderer of 13 Guarded Closely." December 29, 1926, 18.

———. "Slayer of 9 Will Explain Motive." December 27, 1926, 8.

———. "Slayer of 13 Is Happy at Find." February 3, 1927, 1.

———. "Texas Slayer of 9 Will Die in Chair." January 13, 1927, 1.

Nail Rain

Grazulis, Thomas. *Significant Tornadoes 1880–1989*. St. Johnsbury, VT: Environmental Films, 1991.

St. Louis Globe-Democrat. "Mysterious Bombardment of Brownsville." October 17, 1888, 3.

———. "Mysterious Shower of Missiles." October 16, 1888, 1.

Keeping the Peace

Louisville Courier-Journal. "Two Negroes Lynched." November 14, 1891, 5.

Snowing the Officers

Louisville Courier-Journal. "1 Shot Kills 2 in Triple Slaying . . ." December 14, 1925, 1.

———. "Texan Shoots, Beheads His Stepson." December 13, 1925, 1+.

McConal, Jon. "Ancestor Played Role in Head-in-a-Bowl Case." *Fort Worth Star-Telegram*. April 10, 1999.

A Wooly Death

New York Times. "Strange Death of a Woman." July 19, 1888, 5.

You Can't Put One over on the New York Times!

New York Times. "Lynchings in Arkansas." March 25, 1899, 4.

Hill of Heads

New York Times. "A Mound of Human Skulls Found." December 29, 1892, 2.

Odd Oklahoma

Premature Burial

San Francisco Call. "Wealthy Indian Misanthrope Makes Return Trip to Grave." September 18, 1938, I, 11.

Moon's Mania

Louisville Courier-Journal. "Exhumes Wife's Body for Repeated Burials." December 25, 1904, II, 7.

Maurer, Mary. "The Moon Mystery." *Caddo, Oklahoma- My Home Town*. August 29, 2007. http://mem55.typepad.com/caddo_my_home_town/2007/08/index.html.

A Profound Disappointment

Louisville Courier-Journal. "Preacher Is Convicted of Robbing a Grave." November 30, 1912, 7.

Necessity Is the Mother of Invention

Louisville Courier-Journal. "'Bullet-Proof Medicine.'" January 14, 1896, 5.
———. "Inventor Ends Life in Locked Box." February 24, 1932, 1.
———. "Neck Straightener Kills User." March 8, 1939, I, 1.

The Downside of Pioneer Life, Part One

Louisville Courier-Journal. "Tented in a Blizzard." February 14, 1894, 2.

A Real Sense of Comedy Timing

Ardmore [OK] *Daily Ardmoreite*. "Twins Proved Deadly." December 18, 1913, 5.

Theatrical Realism

Louisville Courier-Journal. "Theater Death Chair Kills Electrician." May 26, 1917, 1.

Sincerely, the Corpse

Louisville Courier-Journal. "Officer Signs Suicide Note 'The Corpse.'" November 24, 1936, I, 2.

Miami [OK] *Daily News-Record*. "Army Rites Held at Fort Sill for Suicide." November 26, 1936, 6.

Skinned Alive!

Richardson, W. J. Letter to editor. *Louisville Courier-Journal*. December 4, 1933, 4.

Turnbo, S. C. "Flayed Alive by Indians." Turnbo Manuscripts. Springfield-Green County Library. Accessed July 23, 2018. http://thelibrary.org/lochist/turnbo/V28/ST815.html.

Whitlow, Ozema T. Letter to editor. *Louisville Courier-Journal*. December 9, 1933, 6.

Lend Me Your Ears

Coos Bay Times [Marshfield, OR]. "Kidnappers in Auto Cut Ears." October 20, 1907, 2.

Los Angeles Herald. "Mutilated Corpse Is Evidence of Murder." August 2, 1907, 3.

Louisville Courier-Journal. "Earless Body Identified as Wesley Yandell's." December 11, 1911, 7.

———. "Murderer Cuts off His Victim's Ears." August 2, 1907, 2.

Wichita Daily Eagle. "Find Man's Body in River." March 19, 1907, 2.

———. "Several Identifications." July 24, 1907, 2.

A Stiff Sentence

Daily Oklahoman [Oklahoma City]. "Man Dead for Year Sentenced to 'Pen.'" November 18, 1911, 1.

Louisville Courier-Journal. "Sparks from the Wires." November 18, 1911, 4.

Emma Begs to Differ

Louisville Courier-Journal. "Farm Girl, 18, Kills Father after Tiff." December 22, 1935, I, 1.

———. "Girl Accuses Slain Father." February 25, 1936, 2.

———. "Girl. 18, Freed in Patricide." February 27, 1936, 2.

———. "Girl Freed in Patricide Enters Insane Hospital." February 28, 1936, I, 11.

———. "Girl Who Slew Father Is Freed from Asylum." March 27, 1936, III, 7.

———. "Killer Allowed to Visit Home." December 23, 1935, 2.

An Unseemly Souvenir

Louisville Courier-Journal. "Kidnapper of 2 Texas Cops Dies on Gallows." June 20, 1936, 2.

———. "Mother Sells Nooses to Save Condemned Son." April 4, 1936, 9.

Executions among the Choctaw

Louisville Courier-Journal. "Indian Folsom's Fate." December 26, 1895, 7.

That He Wasn't

Louisville Courier-Journal. "Confesses Killing His Stepmother." July 26, 1012, 7.

Back to Nature

Louisville Courier-Journal. "Skeleton in a Tree." December 20, 1891, 4.

A Hard Day at the Office

Louisville Courier-Journal. "Hanged by the Day." July 22, 1906, I, 4.

Nightmarish Nevada

Bizarre Bequests

Louisville Courier-Journal. "Man Leaves His Beard to Club." January 2, 1927, I, 1.

In a Pickle

Louisville Courier-Journal. "A Body Petrified in Three Years." December 7, 1882, 12.

But Who's Counting?

Florin, Lambert. *Ghost Towns of the West*. New York: Promontory Press, 1971.

Ghosttowns.com. "Pioche." Accessed April 30, 2018. http://www.ghosttowns.com/states/nv/pioche.html.

MacDonald, Craig. "They Didn't Stand a Chance!" *Desert Magazine*, March 1972, 16–17.

Super Skeletons

Brandon, Jim. *Weird America*. New York: Dutton, 1978.

The Trouble with Hairy

Louisville Courier-Journal. "A Strange Creature." November 16, 1879, 2.

Poisoned Potable

New York Times. "Legal Comment on Current Events." March 16, 1930, E6.

What the Hay?

Kentucky Register [Richmond, KY]. "A Man's Body in a Hay Bale." April 15, 1887, 2.

Executions

Louisville Courier-Journal. "Dance Hall Slayer Executed in Nevada." July 14, 1934, 2.

A Meal That Sticks to Your Ribs

Nevada Bob. "Man Unknown." *Find a Grave*. Memorial 24301650. February 1, 2008. https://www.findagrave.com/memorial/24301650/man-unknown.

Numinous North Dakota

Extraordinary Epitaph

Wallis, Charles L. *Stories on Stone*. New York: Oxford University Press, 1954.

One Murder Attempt Too Many

Louisville Courier-Journal. "Poisoned Four Wives." January 15, 1886, 4.

To Avoid Some Work

Louisville Courier-Journal. "Farmer Tells Weird Story of Deaths of 6." December 13, 1930, I, 4.

———. "Father of Man Lynched Gets Life." June 29, 1931, 3.

———. "Father, Son Held in Killing of Six." December 15, 1930, 3.

———. "Young Farmer Admits Slaying 6 in Family." December 14, 1930, I, 1.

A Hasty Trial, and With Good Reason

Bismarck Tribune. "Henry Layer, Murderer of 8, Dies." March 21, 1925, 1+.
Louisville Courier-Journal. "Confesses Murder of Entire Dakota Family." May 14, 1920, 1.
———. "Eight Shot, Hacked to Death . . ." April 25, 1920, I, 1.
———. "Robbers Sought as Slayer of 8." April 26, 1920, 1.

Sure, Why Not?

New York Times. "Could Not Resist Friends." July 28, 1888, 3.

A Dubious Verdict

New York Times. "Dakota's Singular Suicide." January 26, 1884, 1.

Making Their Job Easy

New York Times. "Why She Attempted Suicide." December 17, 1884, 5.

Snowbound

New York Times. "Snowbound on Train for Five Nights." April 3, 1902, 1.

Spooky South Dakota

Encore

Louisville Courier-Journal. "Man Cuts Throat, Swallows Knife." December 23, 1934, I, 8.

Murdering a Monstrosity

Louisville Courier-Journal. "What Was It?" July 17, 1899, 2.

You're a Bad Man, Charlie Brown

Carr, G. Sam. "Swift Justice in Deadwood." *Deadwood Magazine*. 1999. http://www.deadwoodmagazine.com/archivedsite/Archives/swiftjustice.htm.
Louisville Courier-Journal. "A Husband's Revenge." June 19, 1897, 5.

Consolation Prize

Louisville Courier-Journal. "The Vigilantes in the Wild . . ." December 29, 1898, 4.
Sedalia [MO] Democrat. "Cattlemen Who Killed a Sheepherder Make All Restitution Possible." December 28, 1898, 3.

A Community's Revenge

New York Times. "Mob Attacks Wife Beater." August 2, 1908, 10.

Interrupted by the Phone

New York Times. "A Murderer Lynched." April 17, 1885, 2.

Five Mummies

New York Sun. "Entombed Perhaps for Centuries." February 21, 1887, 1.

Unusual Utah

Premature Burial

Pittsburgh Gazette. "A Terrible Fate." July 15, 1874, 2.
Pittsburgh Leader. "Horrible Death of a Boy in Salt Lake Who Was Buried Alive." July 13, 1874, 1.

In a Pickle

Louisville Courier-Journal. "Stuffed Body of Boy in Found in Coffin." August 5, 1934, IV, 7.

Your Typical French Grave-Robbing Hermit

Federal Writers' Project. *Utah: A Guide to the State*. N.p.: Utah State Institute of Fine Arts, 1941.
Shomaker, Joel. "Utah's Ghoulish Scavenger." *Louisville Courier-Journal*, November 10, 1895, II, 4.

Workers United

Louisville Courier-Journal. "Foreigners to Share Grave of Foreman." February 19, 1911, I, 10.

Cult Followings

Louisville Courier-Journal. "Corpse of Cultist Sought in Utah by Health Officials." April 27, 1937, I, 5.
———. "Cult Editor Waits for Wife." May 6, 1937, I, 12.
———. "Cult Expects Body to Come to Life." November 23, 1935, 7.
———. "Cult Head Still Defies Utah in Row Over Body." April 29, 1937, I, 10.
———. "Doctor Launches Campaign to Make Woman Stay Dead." April 25, 1937, I, 20.
———. "Leader of Cult Hints Progress in Reanimation." October 28, 1936, I, 10.

A Dupe Murders a Cad

Louisville Courier-Journal. "Alienists to Be Called." November 23, 1907, 3.
———. "Arthur Brown's Funeral." December 19, 1906, 8.
———. "Bradley Case." Editorial. November 22, 1907, 4.
———. "Brings Tears to Jurors' Eyes." November 20, 1907, 7.
———. "Brown Wrote Many Letters." November 22, 1907, 3.
———. "Case Rests in Hands of Jury." December 3, 1907, 1.
———. "Horse Doctor Could Have Told . . ." December 1, 1907, I, 3.
———. "Insanity Defense of Mr. Bradley." November 16, 1907, 3.
———. "Jury Acquits Mrs. Bradley." December 4, 1907, 3.
———. "Jury Completed." November 15, 1907, 1.
———. "Little Hope." December 11, 1906, 6.
———. "Living in a Hut with Fatherless Babes." January 23, 1908, 1.
———. "Long Wrangle Expected over Testimony." November 24, 1907, IV, 1.
———. "A Man So Unmindful . . ." December 14, 1906, 4.
———. "Mrs. Bradley Held to the Grand Jury." December 14, 1906, 2.

———. "Mrs. Bradley Looked Wild and Haggard." November 19, 1907, 2.
———. "Mrs. Bradley, 'Poor Little . . .'" November 26, 1907, 4.
———. "Mrs. Bradley Seeks Part of Brown's Estate." February 22, 1910, 8.
———. "Mrs. Bradley's Acquittal." December 4, 1907, 4.
———. "No Evidence of Insanity." November 28, 1907, 1.
———. "No Purpose of Revenge." November 21, 1907, 2.
———. "Nothing for the Bradley Children." December 22, 1906, 10.
———. "Put Her in a Padded Cell." November 27, 1907, 4.
———. "Quiet Day in Jail." November 29, 1907, 3.
———. "Sinking Gradually." December 12, 1906, 2.
———. "Suit over Brown Will to Be Settled." September 21, 1910, 4.
———. "Unwritten Law May Decide Case." November 14, 1907, 1.
———. "Was Insane at Time." November 26, 1907, 3.
———. "Week of Experts." November 25, 1907, 3.
———. "Woman's Bullet Proves Fatal." December 13, 1906, 1+.

Remorseful Killers

Louisville Courier-Journal. "Atoning Slayer's Victim Is Found." November 20, 1937, II, 5.
———. "Body Recovered from Well." November 21, 1937, I, 7.
———. "Lone Highwayman Makes Confession." January 11, 1904, 6.
———. "Man Says He Married Woman to Atone . . ." November 18, 1937, I, 11.
Prince, Stephen L. "Antone B. Prince: Washington County Sheriff, 1936–1954." Lecture. St. George Tabernacle, March 27, 2013.

An Uncommonly Stupid Murder

Louisville Courier-Journal. "Headless Body of Girl in Trunk." March 16, 1924, I, 1+.
———. "Insurance Cited in Trunk Slaying." March 17, 1924, 3.
———. "Woman Killed as She Prayed." March 18, 1924, 1.

Lost Treasure, Lost Life

Florin, Lambert. *Ghost Towns of the West*. New York: Promontory Press, 1971.
Thompson, George A., and Fraser Buck. *Treasure Mountain Home: Park City Revisited*. Salt Lake City: Dream Garden Press, 1993.

Abnormal Arizona

Super Skeletons

Louisville Courier-Journal. "Bones of Giant Race Washed Up by Rains." November 27, 1921, IV, 8.

Pickup Service Requested

Casa Grande [AZ] Times. "Man Telephones That He Is Dead . . ." February 28, 1913, 4.

Not a Deadbeat

Louisville Courier-Journal. "An Industrious Ghost." June 1, 1897, 5.

Vintage Violence: Executions and Lynchings

Arizona Republican [Phoenix]. "The End of Hawkins the Tucson Murderer." August 15, 1908, 1.

———. "The Hanging of Hawkins." August 11, 1908, 1.

Louisville Courier-Journal. "Execution of Indian Bungled." July 14, 1936, 2.

———. "Indian, Eager to Hang, Says Judge Is Liar." June 18, 1936, 16.

———. "Kissing Dead Man Causes Wife's Illness." July 11, 1936, 7.

———. "Prison Warden Cruel, Is Charge." December 14, 1924, I, 8.

———. "Slayer's Last Wish Is for Gas Mask." May 15, 1936, I, 4.

New York Times. "Lynch Law in Arizona." August 25, 1873, 5.

———. "Lynching of John Heith [sic]." February 24, 1884, 1.

———. "Mob Recites Prayer Then Hangs Slayer." May 7, 1917, 10.

Gallows Humor

Florin, Lambert. *Tales the Western Tombstones Tell.* New York: Bonanza, 1967.

Dead Man's Drink

Editors of *True West Magazine. True Tales and Amazing Legends of the Old West.* New York: Clarkson Potter, 2005.

Getting Rattled

New York Times. "A Plague of Rattlesnakes." September 23, 1898, 3.

———. "Arizona Snake Stories." September 26, 1898, 3.

Lawson's Leaving

Arizona Republican [Phoenix]. "Blown Out." September 9, 1893, 5.

A Subterranean Swede

Florin, Lambert. *Ghost Towns of the West.* New York: Promontory Press, 1971.

Ed's Humor

Florin, Lambert. *Ghost Towns of the West.* New York: Promontory Press, 1971.

Unnatural New Mexico

Self-Made Monument

Reader's Digest Association, Inc. *Strange Stories, Amazing Facts of America's Past.* Pleasantville, NY: Reader's Digest Association, Inc., 1989.

Billy the Kidnapped?

Louisville Courier-Journal. "The Kid's Body Kidnapped." October 10, 1881, 2.

Tomb Raiders

Louisville Courier-Journal. "Ancient Ghoul Traces Found." October 5, 1924, IV, 4.

Taking a Wrong Turn at Albuquerque

Louisville Courier-Journal. "Death of Pharmacist's Three Former Wives Probed . . ." December 2, 1933, 1.

———. "Druggist Gets Death . . ." April 4, 1934, 2.
———. "Druggist Says He Killed Wife." December 3, 1933, V, 6.

Murder by Horse

Louisville Courier-Journal. "Woman Tied to Broncho and Dragged . . ." October 29, 1911, I, 3.

Those Practical Westerners

Boardman, Mark. "Blowing in the Wind." *True West.* January 13, 2015. https://truewestmagazine.com/blowing-in-the-wind/.

Taking a Dip

Chicago Daily Tribune. "Mystery in Fate of Solomon Luna." August 31, 1912, 7.
New York Times. "New Mexico Favors Wilson." October 13, 1912, 13.

Mr. Kennedy Proves a Bad Host

Florin, Lambert. *Ghost Towns of the West.* New York: Promontory Press, 1971.
Weiser, Kathy. "Charles Kennedy—Old West Serial Killer." *Legends of America.* Last modified April 2017. https://www.legendsofamerica.com/we-charleskennedy/.

Lynchings

Florin, Lambert. *Ghost Towns of the West.* New York: Promontory Press, 1971.
NewMexico.org. "Shakespeare: Ghost Town." Accessed August 29, 2018. https://www.newmexico.org/places-togo/regions-cities/southwest/shakespeare-ghost-town/.
Simmons, Marc. "The Hanging of Russian Bill." *New Mexico Magazine.* October 1980, 68–69.
———. "Socorro Lynch Mob Didn't Wait for Legal Appeal." *Santa Fe New Mexican.* August 9, 2013. http://www.santafenewmexican.com/news/trail_dust/trail-dust-socorro-lynchmob-didn-twait-for-legal/article_01e3e3e5-c49e-57a4-8f5a-9448e73424d1.html.
———. "The Socorro Vigilantes." *New Mexico Magazine.* June 1981, 50–51.

Incredible Idaho

Laughing Last

Louisville Courier-Journal. "Raffles His Tombstone." December 26, 1904, 4.

Ungrateful James

Louisville Courier-Journal. "Boy of 11 to Serve 50 Year Prison Term." December 22, 1912, I, 2.
San Patricio County News [Sinton, TX]. "Boy Convict Plays in Idaho Prison." January 3, 1913, 2.

The Blackest of Black Widows, or: Arsenic and Young Lace

Find a Grave. "Anna Shaw." January 1, 2001. https://www.findagrave.com/cgi-bin/fg.cgi?page=gr&GRid=1484.

Louisville Courier-Journal. "Alleged Husband Slayer Sues for Life Insurance." June 19, 1921, II, 5.
———. "Alleged Slayer of 4th Husband Reaches U.S." June 8, 1921, 7.
———. "Bluebeard Widow, 39, Flees Prison." May 6, 1931, 1+.
———. "Fed Bug Poison to 3 Husbands . . ." October 4, 1921, 2.
———. "Jury, out a Day, Finds Mrs. Southard Guilty." November 5, 1921, 1.
———. "Man to Sue Spouse Who Slew Husband." November 27, 1921, V, 6.
———. "Not Guilty Is Plea of Alleged Husband Killer." June 12, 1921, V, 7.
———. "Poison Found in Body, Experts Say." October 9, 1921, I, 6.
———. "Poisoned Her Four Husbands and Brother of One . . ." September 27, 1921, 1.
———. "Woman Held as Slayer of 6 . . ." May 13, 1921, 1+.
———. "Poisoner of Husband Who Fled From Life Term . . ." August 1, 1932, 1+.
———. "Woman, Mate's Slayer, Gets Ten-Year Term." November 8, 1921, 13.

Mysterious Montana

An Honest Mistake

Daily Missoulian [Missoula, MT]. "Ghouls Still Hold Body of Babe." November 27, 1909, 1.
Louisville Courier-Journal. "Friend Caught in Trap Set for Grave Robbers." May 11, 1911, 2.

Super Skeletons

Louisville Courier-Journal. "Remarkable Fossil Finds in Montana." July 3, 1903, 3.

The Downside of Pioneer Life, Part Two

Louisville Courier-Journal. "A Montana Maniac." August 24, 1890, 5.

Playing and Slaying

Louisville Courier-Journal. "'William Tell' Act Is Fatal to Target." April 27, 1924, II, 1.

Ben's Premonition

Ben Rogers to J. B. Parkes, April 17, 1876, Parkes Family Series, Watts Family Papers, Special Collections and Archives, Crabbe Library, Eastern Kentucky University.
Ben Rogers to J. B. Parkes, March 15, 1876, Parkes Family Series, Watts Family Papers, Special Collections and Archives, Crabbe Library, Eastern Kentucky University.

Vintage Violence: Executions and Lynchings

Glendalemontana.com. "Murder and Mayhem." Accessed July 30, 2018. http://www.glendalemontana.com/murder-and-mayhem.
Kansas City Star, "Tickets to a Hanging $5," October 19, 1902.
Louisville Courier-Journal. "Man Facing Doom Nibbles Orange." February 15, 1925, I, 1.
———. "Promises a Visit from Spirit Land." March 11, 1904, 1.

———. "Tom Salmon's Last Words." January 28, 1899, 3.
New York Times. "Lynched in Jail." March 14, 1883, 2.

From My Cold, Dead Hands

Florin, Lambert. *Ghost Towns of the West*. New York: Promontory Press, 1971.
Metz, Leon Claire. *Encyclopedia of Lawmen, Outlaws, and Gunfighters*. New York: Facts on File, 2002.

Making Do

New Orleans Daily Picayune. "Miscellaneous." April 8, 1909, 2.

Spopee Speaks

Louisville Courier-Journal. "Silence Broken." May 24, 1914, I, 10.
Spokane Daily Chronicle. "Three Decades in Jail; Goes Free." July 7, 1914.

Five Lynched

Florin, Lambert. *Tales the Western Tombstones Tell*. New York: Bonanza, 1967.
Hough, Emerson. *The Story of the Outlaw: A Study of the Western Desperado*. New York: Grosset and Dunlap, 1907.

Domestic Delusion

"Joe Mullery's Remains." *St. Paul Globe*. May 15, 1896, 5.
Whittlesey, Lee H. *Death in Yellowstone*. Boulder: Roberts Rinehart Publishers, 1995.

The Wrong Sausage!

Denver Post. "This Man Ate Sausage He Poisoned for Dog." December 11, 1912, 13.

How Helpful

New York Times. "Dug His Own Grave." May 9, 1891, 1.

The End of a Running Joke

St. Louis Globe-Democrat. "Fatal Result of a Joke." October 18, 1888, 6.

Why It Doesn't Pay to Have Large Hands

New York Times. "'Dead' Man Here; Charge $8,000 Fraud." October 4, 1913, 8.
Wilkes-Barre Times Leader. "Former Local Man Was Murdered." March 24, 1913, 3.

Creepy Colorado

Bizarre Bequests

Louisville Courier-Journal. "Barroom Funeral, Whisky Toast . . ." December 15, 1935, I, 7.
———. "Vengeance, Love Left by Suicide." February 4, 1929, 16.

In a Pickle

Arizona Republican [Phoenix, AZ]. "Preserved Bodies." January 24, 1892, 1.

Body Snatching: The Ultimate Dirty Job
Louisville Courier-Journal. "In a Bad Scrape." May 3, 1889, 1.

A Slight Misdiagnosis
Louisville Courier-Journal. "A Strange Case." December 9, 1881, 2.

Death Diary
Louisville Courier-Journal. "Lived Three Weeks under Snowslide." May 9, 1909, I, 4.

Chain Reaction
Louisville Courier-Journal. "One Pair of Skates Brings Death to 3." January 4, 1936, 2.

A Light at His Feet
Louisville Courier-Journal. "A Ghostly Guardian." December 7, 1884, 13.

Vintage Violence: Executions and Lynchings
Florin, Lambert. *Ghost Towns of the West*. New York: Promontory Press, 1971.
Louisville Courier-Journal. "3 Killers, Good Friends in Death House . . ." May 23, 1935, 1+.
———. "Convicted Murderer Expects to Get Fun . . ." June 21, 1935, I, 1+.
———. "Executed in Cheerful Mood." June 22, 1935, 14.
———. "He Wanted to Jump." February 15, 1886, 5.
———. "Message to Parents Written by Slayer." June 23, 1935, I, 3.
———. "Slayer Denied Request to Die with Friends." May 24, 1935, I, 1.
———. "Tuberculosis Victim Asks to Die . . ." December 31, 1933, I, 1+.
———. "Warden Bans Blind Man from Sensing Execution." September 30, 1939, I, 3.
New York Times. "Banishing Undesirable Citizens." August 2, 1903, 6.
———. "Lynching Husband and Wife." January 20, 1884, 1.
———. "Lynching in Colorado." January 27, 1900, 9.
———. "Reported Lynching in Colorado." August 3, 1900, 3.

An Indian Lynching
Louisville Courier-Journal. "Chinaman Butchered." June 15, 1891, 2.

The Mysterious Denver Strangler
Daily Oklahoma State Capitol [Guthrie]. "The Denver Stranglings." May 10, 1895, 1.
Los Angeles Herald. "Denver Woman Strangled." July 7, 1903, 4.
Louisville Courier-Journal. "The Denver Strangler Mystery." January 7, 1895, 2.
———. "His Third Victim." November 14, 1894, 5.
———. "A Strangler at Work." October 8, 1898, 4.
MacKell, January. *Brothels, Bordellos, and Bad Girls: Prostitution in Colorado, 1860–1930*. Albuquerque: University of New Mexico Press, 2007.
Norman [OK] Transcript. "Stranglers in Denver." November 2, 1894, 6.

A Famished Phantom

Los Angeles Times. "'Ghost' Found in Attic Hideaway Solves Murder." August 1, 1942, 5.

———. "Ghost of Attic Re-enacts Fatal Fight with Friend." August 2, 1942, 28.

San Francisco Chronicle. "The Ghost in the Attic . . ." August 1, 1932, 9.

From the Other Half to the White Hibiscus

Carberry, Jack. "Former Denverite Faces Trial for Life." *Denver Post*, July 28, 1934, 2+.

Denver Post. "Husband Kills College Youth . . ." July 28, 1934, 1.

———. "Poetess in Coast Love Slaying . . ." July 29, 1934, 12.

———. "Poet Had Desire to End Love Affair . . ." July 30, 1934, 25.

———. "Unwritten Law Justified Doke, Jury Declares." December 15, 1934, I, 5.

Louisville Courier-Journal. "Doke Jury Ready." December 7, 1934, 9.

———. "Doke Testifies in Own Defense." November 6, 1934, 3.

———. "Freed Killer of Poet Guilty of $16 Theft." March 8, 1935, 16.

———. "Jury Dismissed in Poet Murder Case." November 10, 1934, 1.

———. "Jury Frees Spouse Who Killed Poet." December 16, 1934, I, 1+.

———. "Killer Sends Wreath to Victim's Funeral." July 29, 1934, I, 10.

———. "Love Letters of Poet Read . . ." November 1, 1934, 1+.

———. "Man Who Killed Poet Is Paroled." May 13, 1938, I, 4.

———. "Premeditation Is Laid to Doke." November 8, 1934, 11.

Culture Clash

Louisville Courier-Journal. "Indian Cleared in Murder of Baby . . ." November 17, 1925, 1+.

———. "Indian Is Held as Live Babe Burier." April 2, 1925, 5.

———. "Medicine Man Gets 15–25 Year Term." April 5, 1925, I, 13.

———. "Medicine Man Slays Cellmate." April 3, 1925, 21.

———. "Ute to Face Trial for Slaying Babe." November 9, 1925, 2.

Murder Most Fowl

Birch, A. G. "Here! Here! Croaks Parrot . . ." *Denver Post*. December 10, 1912, 1+.

Day, John C. "Poor, Failure, and in Old Age . . ." *Denver Post*. December 10, 1912, 1+.

Denver Post. "Parrot Only Double Tragedy Witness . . ." December 13, 1912, 1.

Hutchinson [KS] News. "Facing Poverty . . ." December 11, 1912, 10.

Louisville Courier-Journal. "Kansan Murdered Wife and Committed Suicide." December 11, 1912, 5.

———. "Parrot Answers Not in Murder Case." December 14, 1912, 2.

The Second Item of Business

New York Times. "Leadville Has Jubilee." September 25, 1928, 25.

The Grave That Wasn't

Arizona Silver Belt [Globe, AZ]. "The Grave on Pike's Peak." January 12, 1895, 4.

Hard Luck before and after Death

Florin, Lambert. *Ghost Towns of the West*. New York: Promontory Press, 1971.

A Matter of Civic Pride

Florin, Lambert. *Ghost Towns of the West*. New York: Promontory Press, 1971.

Clifford's Plan

Florin, Lambert. *Ghost Towns of the West*. New York: Promontory Press, 1971.

Way Out Wyoming

Receding Hairlines

Louisville Courier-Journal. "How It Feels to Be Scalped." November 15, 1888, 5.
———. "Scalp Carried by a Redskin." February 17, 1901, III, 3.

A Literal and Figurative Ghost Town

Louisville Courier-Journal. "A Deserted Village." January 26, 1885, 4.

Vintage Violence: Lynchings

Louisville Courier-Journal. "Big-Nose George." March 24, 1881, 3.
———. "Big-Nose George to Be Hanged." December 16, 1880, 3.
———. "Big-Nose George's Crimes." September 15, 1880, 4.
———. "Threats of Hanging Keep Negro's Lynchers Silent," October 3, 1912.
Reader's Digest Association, Inc. *Strange Stories, Amazing Facts of America's Past*. Pleasantville, NY: Reader's Digest Association, Inc., 1989.

A Room with a Boo

Scott, Norman, Michael Scott, and Beth Scott. *Haunted America*. New York: Tor, 1994.
Veit, Rick. Phone interview, March 21, 2017.

Outlandish Oregon

Bizarre Bequests

Louisville Courier-Journal. "Sailor Writes Will in Sea-Going Terms." February 24, 1929, II, 8.

In a Pickle

Louisville Courier-Journal. "Her Body Quickly Turned to Marble." August 29, 1901, 3.

Vintage Violence: Executions

Kansas City Star. "Tickets to a Hanging $5." October 19, 1902.
Louisville Courier-Journal. "Murdered a Man for Twenty-Five Cents." February 1, 1902, 10.

The Pen Is Mightier

Louisville Courier-Journal. "Murder Verdict against Editor." May 22, 1933, 1.

———. "Once Rich Editor Kills Officer . . ." March 17, 1933, 1+.
———. "Publisher Gets Life in Slaying." August 15, 1933, 3.
———. "Slayer Sorry for Victim . . ." March 17, 1933, 1+.

Murder in the Stars

Evening Review [East Liverpool, OH]. "Will Hang on Same Gallows." May 8, 1925, 11.
Jessicado. "Arthur Covell." *Find a Grave*. April 15, 2011. https://findagrave.com/cgi-bin/fg.cgi?page=gr&GRid=68407525.
Louisville Courier-Journal. "Plot to Slay 12 by Astrologer." October 14, 1923, I, 3.

An Early Bigfoot Report?

New York Times. "What Is It?" April 26, 1871, 4.

Weird Washington

Premature Burial

Louisville Courier-Journal. "While Life Was Yet In Him." October 1, 1895, 2.
San Francisco Call. "Pomeroy's Gallows." December 23, 1895, 4.
———. "Pursued by a Mob." March 24, 1893, 2.

Extraordinary Epitaph

Wallis, Charles L. *Stories on Stone*. New York: Oxford University Press, 1954.

In a Pickle

Florence [AZ] Tribune. "Hard as a Mummy." June 1, 1901, 4.

The Portrait That Aged

Louisville Courier-Journal. "The Romance of a Portrait That Changes Every Year." July 16, 1899, III, 5.

Sleep Slaying

Louisville Courier-Journal. "Killed His Wife as He Slept." March 27, 1899, 2.

Good Heads for Business

Florin, Lambert. *Tales the Western Tombstones Tell*. New York: Bonanza, 1967.

Crashing the Party

Louisville Courier-Journal. "4 Men, 2 Women Bound . . ." April 1, 1934, I, 1+.
———. "6 Deaths Sifted." October 26, 1935, 2.
———. "Bloody Suit Lone Clew in Massacre." April 2, 1934, 1+.
———. "Document Seen as Massacre Clew." April 6, 1934, 4.
———. "Girl Accuses Man in 6 Mass Murders of 1934." October 25, 1935, I, 1+.
———. "Jurors Urge Death for Slayer of Six." December 20, 1935, I, 12.
———. "Man Ordered Rearrested in Murder of 6 Persons." April 5, 1934, 2.

In Praise of Mrs. Smith's Superior Housecleaning Skills

Detroit Free Press. "Woman Given Life in Slaying." December 14, 1938, 7.

Louisville Courier-Journal. "Convict Admits 10-Year-Old Slaying." May 8, 1938, I, 6.
———. "Mother, 73, Accuses Son of 4 Murders." May 6, 1938, I, 8.
———. "Mother Pleads with Son to Tell All He Knows . . ." May 9, 1938, I, 5.
———. "Near Perfect Crime Solved by Confession." May 5, 1938, I, 1+.
———. "Nine Murders Laid to Mother and Convict Son." May 13, 1938, I, 4.

An Ugly Incident in a Beautiful Location

Lansing State Journal. "Detective in Gaines Case Held Suicide." August 24, 1926, 7.
Louisville Courier-Journal. "Daughter's Slayer Sentenced to Hang," September 25, 1926, 5.
———. "Father Accused in Girl's Death." June 20, 1926, 1+.
———. "Father of Slain Girl Asks Trail." June 28, 1926, 1+.
———. "Fiend Did Not Kill Girl, View." August 14, 1926, 1+.
———. "Gaines Defense Opens Argument." August 17, 1926, I, 1+.
———. "Gaines' Fate Is in Jury's Hands." August 19, 1926, 1.
———. "Gaines Guilty, Death Is Asked." August 20, 1926, 1.
———. "Gaines Prober Thought Slain." August 24, 1926, 4.
———. "Girl, 22, Is Found Strangled to Death." June 18, 1926, 1.

The Unanswered Question

Louisville Courier-Journal. "Bail Secured for Accused Doctor." September 28, 1926, 4.
———. "Dr. Moore Faces Suit for $25,000." December 31, 1926, 1.
———. "Jury Sought to Try Dr. Moore." November 16, 1926, 22.
———. "Moore Is Freed in Wife's Death." November 20, 1926, 1.
———. "Plot Charged by Accused Doctor." September 6, 1926, 1+.
———. "State Blocked in Moore Trial." November 18, 1926, 1.
———. "U. of L. Graduate Held in Wife's Death." September 5, 1926, I, 1+.
———. "Witness Accuses Moore in Trial." November 17, 1926, 1.

George's Jig

San Francisco Examiner. "Swallows Poison and Dances . . ." October 7, 1904, 15.

An Ounce of Prevention Is Worth a Body in a Tree

New York Times. "A Desperado Lynched." February 21, 1885, 1.

Mr. Tracy Goes Camping

Louisville Courier-Journal. "Bloodhounds Track Tracy." July 14, 1902, 4.
———. "Bloody Bandages." July 17, 1902, 1.
———. "Blots out Remarkable Career with His Own Hand." August 7, 1902, 1+.
———. "Desperado Gives Desperate Battle." July 4, 1902, 1+.
———. "Desperado Tracy's Record Since June 9 Last." August 7, 1902, 3.
———. "Frank James Says Only One Way . . ." August 3, 1902, I, 7.
———. "Fugitive Tracy." August 2, 1902, 1.
———. "Given Slip Again." July 18, 1902, 1.
———. "Hold-Up of a Family . . ." July 11, 1902, 1.
———. "Inquest over Body of Tracy." August 8, 1902, 2.
———. "Leaves a Note." August 6, 1902, 1.
———. "Man Hunt Off." July 20, 1902, I, 6.

———. "No Clews of Tracy Since He Left Cabin." July 19, 1902, 1.
———. "Off the Track." July 10, 1902, 1.
———. "Only an Accident Will Reveal Hiding Place." July 6, 1902, I, 7.
———. "On Trail." July 9, 1902, 1.
———. "Outlaw Tracy Reported to Have Been Seen Crossing . . ." July 16, 1902, 1.
———. "Pursuers Again Eluded . . ." July 7, 1902, 1.
———. "Questions and Answers." August 24, 1902, III, 8.
———. "Seen But Keeps On." August 3, 1902, I, 4.
———. "A Somewhat Benevolent Bandit." March 11, 1912, 5.
———. "Still at Large." July 5, 1902, 3.
———. "Still Elusive." July 15, 1902, 4.
———. "Told the Actress He Was Outlaw Tracy." July 29, 1902, 4.
———. "Tracy Looks Fresh and Is Not Wounded." July 24, 1902, 1.
———. "Tracy's Remains Received." August 10, 1902, I, 2.
———. "Two Men's Tracks . . ." July 8, 1902, 2.
———. "Wanted His Leg Exhumed." June 25, 1916, I, 10.
———. "Wounded Outlaw Tracy Staggers Ahead of Posse." July 13, 1902, III, 1.

Keven McQueen is Senior Lecturer in the Department of English at Eastern Kentucky University. He is the author of numerous books, including *Horror in the Heartland* and *Creepy California*.

www.ingramcontent.com/pod-product-compliance
Lightning Source LLC
Chambersburg PA
CBHW050015090426
42734CB00021B/3283